HOW TO GET THE BEST FROM YOUR COFFEE

A BOOK ABOUT BREWING
BY PETE LICATA

Copyright © 2019 Pete Licata

All rights reserved. No part of this publication may be reproduced, distributed, or transmitted in any form or by any means, including photocopying, recording, or other electronic or mechanical methods, without the prior written permission of the publisher, except in the case of brief quotations embodied in critical reviews and certain other noncommercial uses permitted by copyright law. For permission requests, contact Pete Licata.

ISBN: 978-0-6486544-1-4 (Print)

Edited by Chris Ryan
Design & illustration by Cindy Ondrick

First edition 2019

www.licatacoffeeconsultants.com

TABLE OF CONTENTS

Preface 7

My Brew Recipe 11

Brew Fundamental 1: Water 19

Brew Fundamental 2: Device & Filter 33

Brew Fundamental 3: Grinding........................... 53

Brew Fundamental 4: Variables.......................... 69

Conclusion: Happy Brewing 89

Glossary 91

Acknowledgments 93

PREFACE

It's the first day of the Cafe Show in Seoul, South Korea, with thousands of specialty-coffee devotees milling about on the packed show floor. I've arrived from a long transcontinental flight only hours before, and the jet lag I'm battling is hard to ignore. But I have to focus on the task at hand.

I'm behind a table at a well-known coffee roasting company's booth, and I am charged with brewing coffee for the curious attendees who stop by. There are brewing devices set out before me and I'm filling the water kettle when the booth attendant hands me the coffee. It's a natural-processed Ethiopia that is capable of tasting super-fruity, complex, and beautiful.

However, this specific coffee has been unfamiliar to me before this very moment, and it's roasted quite a bit lighter than the coffees I would typically brew at home. I'm tasked with doing justice to this coffee, but I'm in unfamiliar territory, and I need to use some ingenuity to produce a brew that will do justice to the people who grew, processed, and roasted this coffee, as well as please the curious people stopping by the booth.

This scenario is probably familiar to many baristas and coffee professionals— maybe you weren't at a trade show, but you could have been in your family's kitchen at Thanksgiving, when you were handed a new coffee and were asked to make it taste amazing. If you are like me, you get high expectations from friends and family because you are "the expert."

As any barista knows, proper extraction is the key to brewing coffee that tastes delicious—or, in other words, to brewing a cup that reaches the optimal flavor level for that particular coffee. In a situation like the one I've just described where we baristas can't change our coffee, we simply must alter our extraction techniques to create the best cup for our consumers.

We all have opinions on what "ideal" coffee is, but I believe that we can get the best version out of any specialty coffee regardless of its roast, elevation, or other factors as long as it is relatively free of defects. Because I have been in a position to work with coffee in a widely varied range, it has given me time to rethink my approach to coffee extraction. As a result, I have found incredible versions of coffees that I would have simply dismissed a few years ago.

Somewhere along the line in my coffee experimentation journey, it occurred to me that my approach to creating a brew recipe would be a compelling topic for a book. I've done a lot of trial and error—and made many cups of coffee ranging from undrinkable to unbelievably delicious. But I have come out the other side with a tried-and-true brewing method that I think is useful to anyone who brews coffee on a regular basis.

I'm very excited to share the product of my brewing research with the greater community via this book. I view this project as another step in understanding the ideas behind extracting coffee. What we have traditionally left up to simple measurements and basic tasting expectations is now turning to scientific study and ever-more-detailed understandings about how and why some coffee tastes amazing and other coffee tastes ... less amazing.

What I will be presenting in the following pages is a combination of my methods, thought processes, and concepts in regard to the extraction of "filter" coffee made with manual pour-over devices that commonly use paper filters. We won't get into immersion and mechanical batch brewing, nor will we cover espresso brewing; there are so many specific elements to be considered in these different fields that exploring them would send us too far off course. Maybe these will be topics for future books!

This book is presented in an uncommon format. I will give you my specific method first, and then explain the reasoning and some handy experiments in the following chapters. Why did I organize the book this way? It's simple: Everyone wants the "how" when they first pick up a book, and there is no reason to waste your time flipping to the back to find it.

THE 4 FUNDAMENTALS OF BREWING

The details of "why" that follow are highly valuable though, so you really, really need to read them! (They are presented as the four "fundamentals" following the brew recipe.) In addition, I have conducted experiments that you can easily replicate in your own cafe or home. I find that the value of experimentation is largely in the hands-on participation, and so I highly encourage you to try the experiments contained in this book to further your knowledge and taste firsthand what I'm talking about.

Thank you for purchasing this book; bringing it to you has been an endeavor in organization and patience, and has required me in many ways to redefine what I thought I knew. Working in the specialty-coffee industry, we all must continually grow, learn, and push the boundaries of the ordinary. Because specialty has historically been a niche of the larger coffee industry, we have had to define ourselves and show that the product can truly be different from the norm. Without this effort to grow, we would not be the successful industry that we are.

Please enjoy the brewing recipe, details, and experiments contained in these pages. I hope that through the lessons shared here, you will experience fewer pitfalls in your brewing journey than I have in mine.

Thanks for reading,

Pete Licata

MY BREW RECIPE

Here it is, my method for creating a brew recipe! (You didn't even have to search for it.) Honestly, reading this chapter and looking at the accompanying chart probably won't blow your mind in terms of making a standard filter brew. Everything is presented in a purposeful order, and while most of this should be at least familiar to you, the specific reasoning for each component is in the details. (This is another reason I want you to read the rest of the book!)

If you utilize the following methodology in your brewing, you will find solid, consistent, and repeatable results using coffees of all stripes. The implementation of proper methods is in some ways more important than knowing all of the details of why you do each step.

To begin, let's choose a coffee to help illustrate the recipe more clearly. Let's go with a washed Peruvian coffee, Typica variety, grown around 1,500-1,600 meters above sea level, roasted to a "medium" roast. This is a simple yet delicious coffee when brewed properly.

Now let's get into it:

1. Make sure you have good water.

Your water should abide by Specialty Coffee Association standards. We don't need magic-formulation water, but we do need our water to be good and consistent—basically, it should have a neutral flavor that doesn't interfere with the taste of your coffee, as well as a reasonable level of dissolved minerals. If you don't have a good source for water, local bottled spring water may work. Other options include Third Wave Water packets or Peak Water filtration, to name just a couple. Make sure your water has a reasonable TDS (ideally 75-250 mg/l), no odors, and especially no chlorine/chloramine (which will kill your brew).

2. Measure your coffee's whole-bean density in g/cl to determine the water temperature.

This is probably a new step for you, but it's important to measure the density of whole-bean roasted coffee, as there is a direct correlation between a coffee's density and how much thermal energy is needed to extract its more desirable flavor elements. I use a 25-centiliter (cl) graduated cylinder to test density. To measure your coffee's density, fill your vessel to a known volume and weigh it. (You can achieve that known volume by filling a vessel to the top with water and weighing it; the gram weight of water is approximate to milliliters of volume.) Divide the weight of your coffee by the volume it filled in centiliters. So in the case of our Peru coffee, let's do the math: 25cl of whole-bean roasted coffee weighs 95.3g. Next divide 95.3(g) by 25(cl). The quotient of this equation is 3.812(g/cl). The hard part is done! Now just reference the handy chart (see **Figure 1**) to determine your water set temperature. For our Peruvian coffee, the water set temperature will be 198°Fahrenheit.

DENSITY TO TEMPERATURE

DENSITY (G/CL)	BREWING TEMPERATURE
3.500	195°F / 90.5°C
3.600	196°F / 91.1°C
3.700	197°F / 91.6°C
3.800	198°F / 92.2°C
3.900	199°F / 92.7°C
4.000	200°F / 93.3°C
4.100	201°F / 93.8°C
4.200	202°F / 94.4°C
4.300	203°F / 95.0°C
4.400	204°F / 95.5°C
4.500	205°F / 96.1°C
4.600	206°F / 96.6°C

The temperatures on this chart are for a manual pouring kettle set temperature, not the temperature of the slurry itself.

Figure 1

3. Select an appropriate brew device and filter paper.

You might have a preference on the brewing device you use. When choosing a coffee dripper, its shape, the material it is made from, and the filter options available for that design will have a big impact on the finished cup. Plastic and metal drippers are durable, but there's a drop-off in extraction efficiency compared to ceramic drippers. The quality and thickness of the filter paper will affect the amount of solids that make it into the cup, which will further influence the flavor of the brewed coffee. My current preference is a ceramic Hario V60 dripper for its heat retention, and standard V60 white filters to increase the extraction yield in the cup overall.

4 Grind appropriately for the brew device.

The grind of your coffee is responsible for allowing efficient extraction when water hits it, slowing the overall flow of liquid exiting the filter and creating complexity in the cup. A common grind suggestion for a V60 is "medium-fine," but that is a very general term, and we'll get into a more detailed description in the pages ahead. Your V60 grind should allow for a finished extraction time of between 2 minutes 30 seconds and 3 minutes, including a 30-second bloom and full draw-down through the grinds. The timing is a reflection of your overall dose and brew amount. My basic recipe is 18g of coffee, which brews in 2 minutes 30 seconds. A dose of 25g may have a 3-minute complete brew time, and often requires a slightly coarser grind.

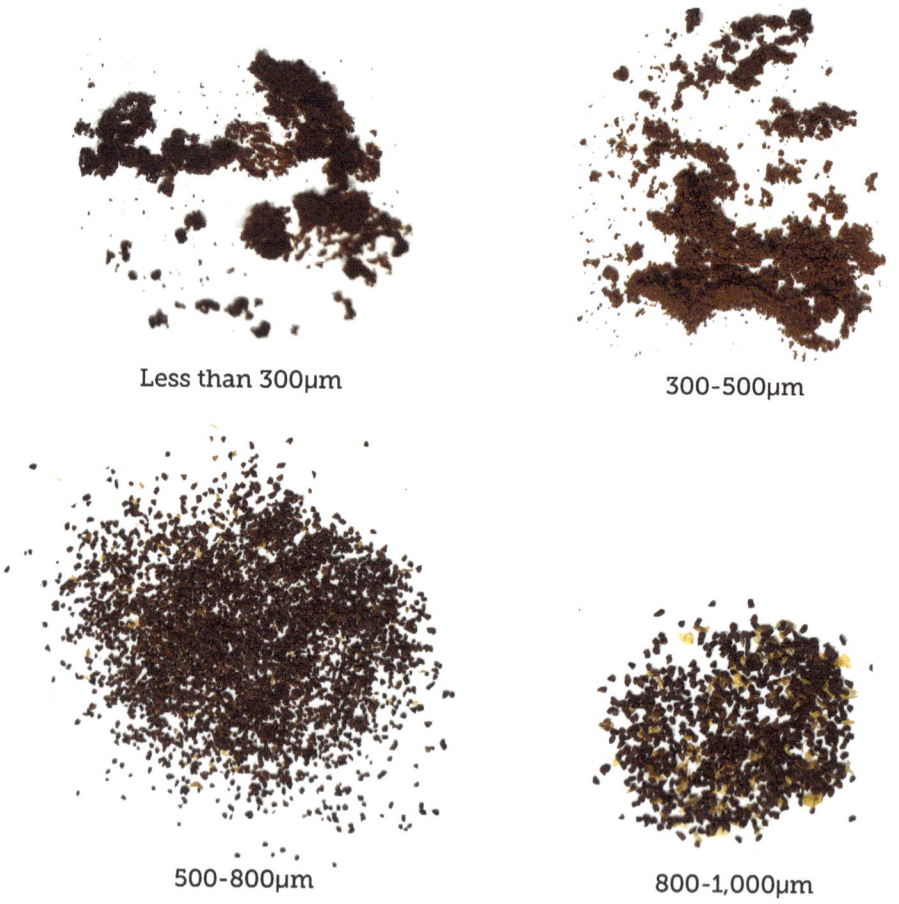

Less than 300µm   300-500µm

500-800µm   800-1,000µm

5 Select your brew ratio.

Your brew ratio is directly tied to the strength of the cup, and is typically conveyed in grams of coffee to grams of water weight. A smaller ratio (e.g., 1:13) will make a strong cup of coffee, but may result in under-extraction as well as a muddled flavor experience. A bigger ratio (e.g., 1:20) will make a weak, even watery cup of coffee with a potential over-extraction or muting of flavor qualities. Generally, more balanced extractions tend to be in the middle of these examples. My preference is always close to 1:16.5, with some fluctuation based on extremely light or dark roasts. A moderate brew ratio, in combination with the other factors presented in this recipe, tends to result in full extraction (19-21% yield), well-articulated flavors, and balance of the major coffee characteristics. If we start with an 18g dose, we should be using 300g of water for a 1:16.5 ratio. (18g times 16.5 equals 297g, but I rounded it up to 300g for a nice even number—it won't noticeably affect the flavor of the brew.)

START WITH 1:16.5

6 Brew considering turbulence and agitation concerns.

Turbulence and agitation come into play whenever we pour water aggressively or actively stir with a spoon or other implement. I use a few different pouring methods at different stages of the coffee-brewing process for best results. Pouring aggressively, for example, introduces water more forcefully to the coffee, creating a lot of active mixing between grinds and water. Low-turbulence center pouring, on the other hand, slowly introduces water to the brew, causing minimal interaction between grinds and water.

To put it simply, turbulence will increase the rate of extraction in your slurry, which is great for getting more flavor out of the coffee. It can easily become too much extraction, however, which will result in bitter or astringent flavors. With a ceramic V60, I prefer aggressive pouring on the initial 50g of water after the bloom, followed by low-impact center pouring, and the final 50g of water being turbulent again in a circular motion in order to free enough fines to slow the final draw-down. My standard method for an 18g dose with 300g water is: bloom 40g > turbulent pour 50g > steady center pour 160g > turbulent clockwise pour 50g. Try to finish pouring water by 1 minute 30 seconds to 1 minute 45 seconds.

 LET'S TALK ABOUT REFRACTOMETERS

In tracking the data from the tests I conducted for this book, I used a refractometer, a scientific tool that identifies extraction amounts and measures a coffee's concentration.

I find refractometers to be useful for simple analysis and for better understanding the process of coffee extraction. Do I think you must use one when you brew? Absolutely not. If you are confident that you can taste your ideal brew strength and are hitting the standard range of extraction from your coffee without one of these tools, then by all means go without it.

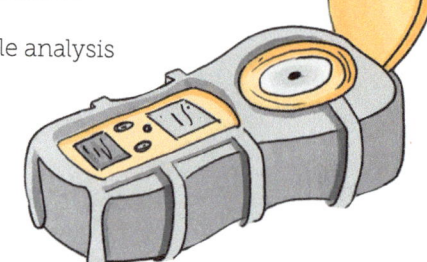

7

Taste and refine if needed.

Measurement tools—like the aforementioned refractometer—can help you see where your brew fits into a general range, but our tongues still should do the heavy lifting in terms of identifying a great flavor experience. At this point, taste your coffee to identify if your method needs adjustment. If the brew time was fast, try a finer grind. If the final draw-down took too long and/or there is a mild bitterness, try using less turbulence/agitation. If you feel the flavor is weak, try a smaller brew ratio or a slightly finer grind. If the flavor is compressed or strong, try a longer brew ratio or a slightly coarser grind. Once you get the hang of this method, your adjustments should become minimal and more intuitive.

Remember that if you change one variable, it will have an impact on the others. For example, if you increase your dose (and of course your brew water), your brew time will go up and you may need a coarser grind. If you use less turbulence/agitation, your final brew time may be faster due to fewer fines getting trapped in the filter. Give yourself a couple of tries to get a feel for the method, and when you're curious about the specifics of each fundamental, dig into the corresponding chapters for more details!

BREW FUNDAMENTAL ONE

You've likely heard the old adage, "Coffee is 99% water." While in reality that number may be more like 98.5%, the sentiment of the saying rings true: Water plays a vital role in our beverage, so in order to make great-tasting coffee, we must pay close attention to our water as the first step to a successful brew recipe.

I have broken this section up into two parts: first some basics on water chemistry, then a look at water temperature. The goal is to understand a bit about how water works and the minerals affecting its flavor before we jump into choosing temperatures to produce the best brew.

Without further ado, let's jump back to high school for a quick chemistry lesson.

WATER CHEMISTRY

The chemistry of water is a complex topic to tackle. In my experience, the more you understand, the more complicated the subject becomes. So this will not be an exhaustive deep dive into water chemistry; rather, we'll hit some key points that will help us fine-tune our water so that it enhances our brew rather than detracts from it.

When it comes to what's in our water, we know we need a small amount of dissolved mineral solids—without them, our brews are off-balance and unpredictable—and we have an understanding of what some of those minerals do to impact the finished brew. Magnesium, calcium, and bicarbonate are the main elements of our magical water, which produce high-quality flavor results when combined with coffee.

Magnesium has the strongest impact on overall extraction—when present in small amounts, it makes dissolvable solids more extractable, which can help bring out the acids and sharp flavors from coffee (as discussed in *Water for Coffee* by Maxwell Colonna-Dashwood and Christopher Hendon). However, too much magnesium (>500 mg/l) may have a negative effect on the brew flavor.

Calcium also has an impact on the extraction of coffee, though a bit less than magnesium. It is considered to be responsible for raising sweetness and body in the brew process, but that comes with a caveat: Too much calcium in your water can lead to a chalky taste, and if excess calcium is present along with extra carbonates, it will likely create limescale on the interior of your heating device.

Bicarbonate/carbonate is considered a "buffer," which means it regulates the acid levels in coffee. It does this by attaching itself to excess acid molecules, lowering our perception of bright or sharp flavors (like the ones that magnesium extracts) and making our coffee more palatable.

CREATE YOUR OWN WATER CHEMISTRY

While it may be impractical for most cafes or individuals to tailor a specific water chemistry to an individual coffee to match the origin/roast/extraction, this does happen, most commonly in the Brewers Cup competition. (However, barista competitions such as the one I'm most familiar with, the World Barista Championship, do not allow competitors to alter the chemistry of their water.) If you are interested in a specific water composition to test out with a certain coffee, perhaps for building a Brewers Cup routine, I personally find a ratio of 2 parts magnesium, 2 parts calcium, 1 part bicarbonate in pure water to be quite desirable, with a TDS between 75-150 mg/l. This also lets us better taste what is actually in the cup.

Maxwell Colonna-Dashwood, our friendly water expert, describes the buffer's role like this: "Coffee is mildly acidic, and the buffer cancels out the acidic compounds by turning them into the non-acidic version of themselves, called conjugate partners," he says. "The thing about the buffer is it can change the cup profile dramatically after extraction. A really easy way to see this is to brew a cup of coffee and then drop a tiny pinch of baking soda (sodium bicarbonate) and watch all of the acidity in the flavor profile disappear."

Hence, too much bicarbonate in the water can overwhelm the resulting brew, but a reasonable amount will create a more palatable cup.

Practical solutions to the problem(s) with water

Knowing which minerals are vital to a great brew is key, but a big reason water chemistry has been difficult to standardize is that every water source, in every city around the world, has a different amount of dissolved mineral solids readily available. Some cities have very high levels of minerals, while others' levels are very low. Some cities' water supplies have undesirable components that need to be filtered out, while others' are fantastic with minimal filtration.

On the bright side, it has become considerably easier in the past decade to determine what's in your city's water supply; the internet has made public water information much more accessible. The question then becomes: Once we know what's in our water, how do we eliminate the elements we don't want while keeping what we *do* want?

The simplest answer to that question is: Get a filtration system. More specifically, find a system within your budget that provides **good-quality water (odor-free, clean, and free of contaminants); a consistent mineral profile; and a reasonable total mineral level (TDS)**, in that order of priority. Options for filtration systems vary wildly, but here are some different routes that may make sense depending on whether you're a business or an individual—and how much money you're able to spend.

For the cafe. If you are working on water for a cafe or large-capacity business, you will probably need either a reverse-osmosis system—which uses water pressure to force out contaminants—or a series of filters to remove specific elements. The cost of top-quality filtration can be high, but it is a necessary investment to pull off a great coffee program.

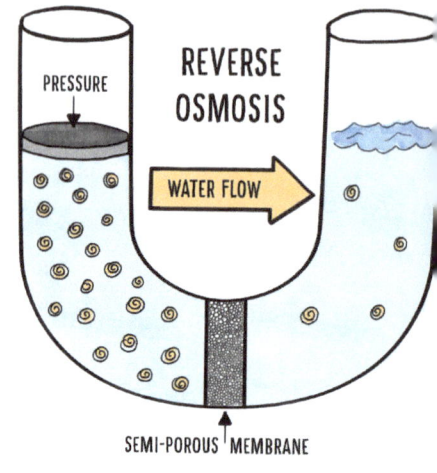

Your specific approach will likely depend on your local source of water and how consistent it is throughout the year. For example, in my hometown of Kansas City, the water tends to be quite hard—meaning it has higher-than-desired levels of calcium and/or magnesium dissolved in it—and has a little bicarbonate from the local water table. So cafes in the area often implement a reverse-osmosis system with a bypass to allow small amounts of tap water through.

Unfortunately, because Kansas City's water source draws in part from the rivers—and the quality of the water fluctuates when there is a lot of rain—coffee businesses must frequently take the extra step of adjusting how much they use that bypass to regulate the TDS of the water. There are also times when the mineral components completely change, especially when heavy rains cause river flooding in the area; when that happens, shops may need a remineralization system that actively dissolves small amounts of minerals back into the water. Remineralization systems are often also used by coffee businesses in cities where the mineral content of the water coming from the tap is very low to begin with.

For home. If you are brewing at home or on a very small scale, purchasing a reasonable spring water or a water filter is likely all you need to do—one good option for the latter is the Peak Water jug, an invention by Maxwell Colonna-Dashwood and Christopher Hendon that removes the undesirable components of tap water but leaves enough good minerals in the water. Another option is Third Wave Water, a mineral packet that can be added to water to create the ideal formula for coffee brewing (and while they started out being geared toward the home user, they're now providing water solutions for the cafe as well!).

Water chemistry takeaways

For the aforementioned reasons of complexity and the immense depth that this single topic can go to with coffee, once you find a good source of water that is consistent, don't worry too much about further changing your water chemistry. Fortunately, recent studies (Google "The Science of Perfect Water for Coffee" for an example) indicate that the actual amount of total dissolved solids in water is less important to making a great brew than having enough minerals in the right proportions. So again, get that good supply and stick with it. There are tons of other brewing variables that are much more useful to focus on.

I don't want to insinuate that water chemistry is not important, but unless you have a background in the subject, jumping into it may just cause more confusion than benefit. If you do want to wade deeper into the subject of water, I highly suggest you pick up Maxwell and Christopher Hendon's book, *Water for Coffee*.

TEMPERATURE CONVERSIONS

I've included temperatures in Fahrenheit because it's what I grew up using in Kansas City. If you're used to seeing your temperatures in Celsius, I suggest using a simple Fahrenheit-to-Celsius converter online. But if you prefer to do the conversions by hand, the conversion formula is C = 5/9 (F - 32). So for example, if the temperature is 86°F, we replace F in the formula with 86, and the result is 30°C.

WATER TEMPERATURE

Now that we've covered the basics of water chemistry and you've decided you have a good, consistent source of water, we can talk about your water temperature.

When brewing coffee, you need to heat your kettle so the water will be ready to go after you've prepped your other brewing needs. So how do you determine a starting point for brew temperature? The SCA's recommended range of water temperature for coffee brewing is 195°F to 205°F. Do you just start at 200°F—a safe number in the middle of that range—and go from there?

While that approach could result in a decent brew, I prefer to take a different tact. My method for recipe creation points straight to an ideal brew temperature first, which is vital in extracting just enough of a coffee's flavor without hitting over-extracted characteristics such as dryness, astringency, and bitterness. By setting an "ideal" temperature, you will have a guiding baseline to make an excellent cup, and you can tweak your grind and technique to further fine-tune your results—we'll talk about that more in future chapters.

In this section, I'll explore how temperature impacts extraction and look at how we set our ideal temperature through an important factor called bean density.

A NOTE ABOUT TESTING METHODOLOGY

I conducted all of the experiments featuring extracted coffee in this book with coffee brewed directly from the device, as I think this is the best way to compare the liquid in any given cup. While some brew tests use a secondary filter—typically a fine syringe filter—before measuring TDS and extraction yield, I believe a filter brew has no need for additional filtering, so I did not use a secondary filter for the tests.

Temperature and extraction

Heated water is arguably the most powerful component of coffee extraction. The stored energy within hot water quickly and efficiently pulls out the many compounds of coffee during brewing, with the resulting extraction impacted by additional factors such as grind size and the overall surface area of the grinds the water contacts.

While the SCA has its aforementioned recommended range of water temperature to properly extract coffee, there is no consensus from coffee professionals about which water temperature should be used for a specific brew, largely because there are varying degrees of understanding on how and why temperature should be changed.

So what do we know about how temperature impacts extraction? For one, we know that the hotter the brewing water is, the more solids (i.e., what TDS reads) the

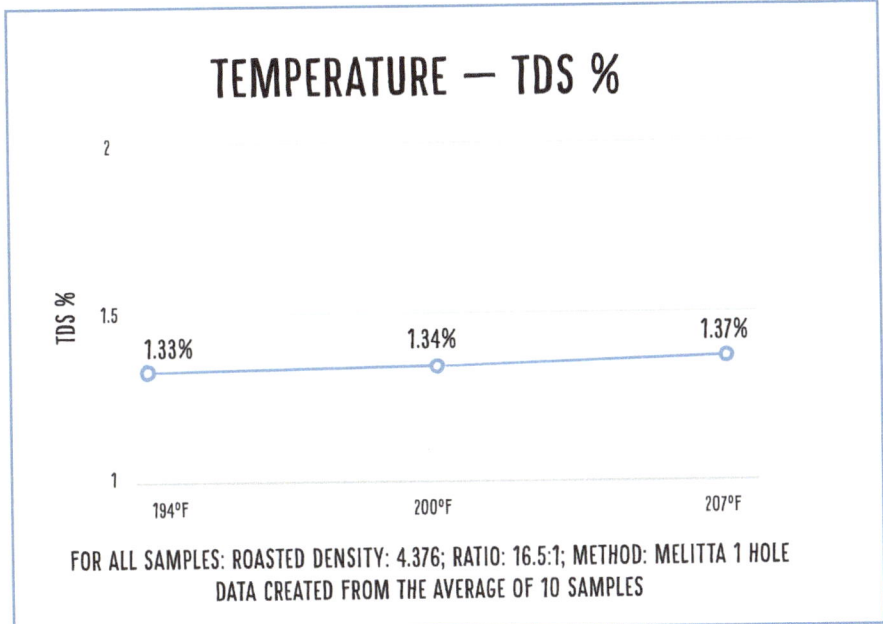

Figure 2

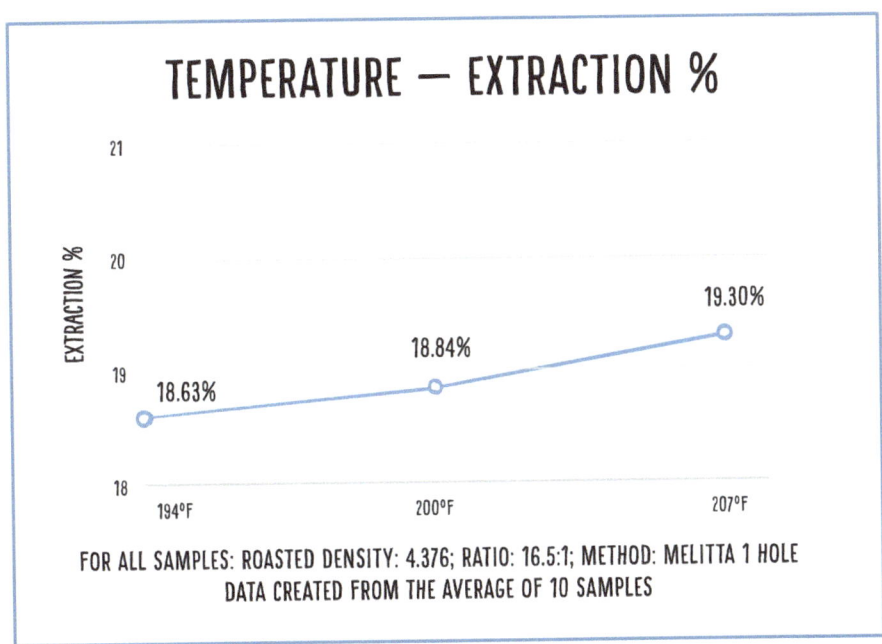

Figure 3

water will typically extract from a coffee. This can be seen in **Figures 2 and 3** as simple correlations between the brewing temperature and the overall TDS and extraction yield.

Additionally, esteemed specialty-coffee professional Ted Lingle—in his book *The Coffee Brewing Handbook*—tells us that higher temperatures, generally speaking, are capable of extracting complex carbohydrates and resilient acids, both of which contribute to a balanced cup when present in a coffee. Lower temperatures, on the other hand, are less likely to extract these tougher compounds (usually because they're bigger molecules), but are still capable of dissolving sugars, salts, and more readily available organic acids. These simpler compounds are a necessity for creating a tasty cup of coffee with a good extraction level.

When, then, does it make sense to use higher and lower temperatures to brew coffee? Choosing your water temperature will largely be dictated by how your coffee is roasted, as that determines what components the coffee may possess that you'll want to bring out. By that logic, one might reason that lighter-roasted coffee should be brewed with hotter water, and darker-roasted coffee with cooler water. While there is certainly some sense to that approach, I don't think it's quite that straightforward.

Rather, I believe there is a more exact way to determine ideal brewing temperature. To get a better snapshot of your coffee—and in turn determine the proper temperature at which to brew it—I would suggest measuring its roasted, whole-bean density.

Understanding temperature through density

Density has been a rather ambiguous term in the coffee world that is generally used in reference to the harder, heavier beans that come from high-altitude farms i.e., dense beans). I want you to forget about density in this way, and instead think of it as a measurement of coffee's weight versus its physical volume. For the purposes of a consistent metric, I will only be talking about a density number in terms of grams per centiliter (g/cl)—but we'll come back to that shortly.

I have discovered measuring whole-bean density to be the best way to correlate a consistent temperature at which a coffee should be brewed. This may go against everything that you feel you know about how coffee should be extracted—typically coffee pros start at 200°F and adjust from there based on what they taste. But I think this measurement is a surefire way to achieve a great cup with a wide variety of coffees.

Before we proceed, let's ask a basic question: What exactly do we mean by "density" in coffee beans? This measurement is a reflection of how much moisture is in the beans, how tightly packed the cell structure of the beans is, and how big the beans are on average. You can think of density and heaviness as synonyms: A more moist, more tightly packed, and smaller bean will be denser/heavier. The opposite is true of less dense/lighter coffees.

A coffee's density is determined by many factors, starting at origin when the cherry is picked from the tree—a ripe, red cherry indicates the bean inside has fully developed, which will provide the ideal window for great flavor and consistent density. The processing method chosen by the producer also has an impact on the final density of the green bean. For example, a coffee that was washed and dried over seven to 10 days tends to have a higher green bean density than that same coffee being dried in the fruit for a full month. Fruit drying allows more time for the seed to germinate and break down the cell structure as the seed is preparing to grow into a new plant, potentially lowering the density of the bean.

Brew Fundamental 1: WATER

While these green-coffee practices will influence a bean's density potential, by far the biggest factor on density is the roasting process, in which the beans will quickly lose water weight and their cell structure will further degrade. In general terms, a faster roast time with a low final roast temperature will result in less water-weight loss than a longer roasting time and/or high roast temperature, resulting in a higher density. The higher the roast degree (final temperature), the more the beans will tend to expand in size, dry out, and subsequently have a more fragile cell structure, lowering the density. Roasting is an incredibly complex process with seemingly limitless variability potential, but let's sum it up to say that the more energy inputted to the coffee during roasting, the more potential there is for a loosening of the cell structure and loss of water, and in turn a lower density.

Ideally, a coffee will be roasted in such a way that honors the integrity of the coffee created at origin. But in reality, the roasting preference dictates the end result—if a low-density green coffee has been roasted extremely light and short, it may well be more dense than a high-density green coffee that was roasted too long or hot.

For this reason, it only makes sense to measure the density of a coffee for extraction purposes after it is roasted and whole bean.

Before we move on to measuring density for your brew recipe, I think it's worth clarifying that this measurement is not a determining factor of a coffee's quality.

As I've discussed, you can have higher- and lower-density coffees as a result of many factors—the roasting technique and process first and foremost—but you can brew a delicious cup with beans from a range of densities. The key to achieving this is matching the bean density to the correct water temperature.

Putting density into brewing action

By measuring the density (in the aforementioned grams per centiliter metric) of whole-bean roasted coffee, we can create a primary sliding scale for coffee extraction. Taking this one measurement will allow you to cut out a significant number of steps in the process of "dialing in" a coffee for its best extraction.

As mentioned in the brew recipe, to calculate grams per centiliter, use a 25cl graduated cylinder and weigh the full 25cl in grams. To get the density reading, you simply divide the gram weight by 25(cl). The resulting number will typically be between 3.500g/cl and 4.500g/cl for most specialty coffees, though occasionally we find some coffees outside of this range. Figure 1 directs you straight to a set of corresponding density readings and water temperatures. If your result number is between a set (i.e., 3.965g/cl), it is usually best to round up or down to whichever round density number is closest.

DENSITY TO TEMPERATURE

DENSITY (G/CL)	BREWING TEMPERATURE
3.500	195°F / 90.5°C
3.600	196°F / 91.1°C
3.700	197°F / 91.6°C
3.800	198°F / 92.2°C
3.900	199°F / 92.7°C
4.000	200°F / 93.3°C
4.100	201°F / 93.8°C
4.200	202°F / 94.4°C
4.300	203°F / 95.0°C
4.400	204°F / 95.5°C
4.500	205°F / 96.1°C
4.600	206°F / 96.6°C

The temperatures on this chart are for a manual pouring kettle *set temperature*, not the temperature of the slurry itself.

Figure 1

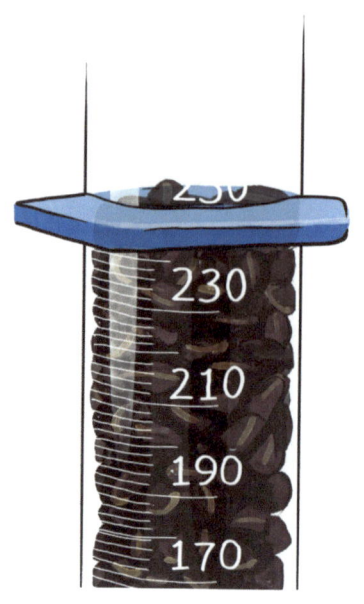

I do want to acknowledge that this density reading is not infallible. There are certain types of coffees that may behave outside of the norm here, such as the tiny Mokka variety grown on Maui, robusta coffees, or even decaffeinated samples. While we may find outliers from the norm, my testing of density in relation to temperature has been ongoing with no major departures from the chart in this book. I highly encourage you to stick with the chart to begin dialing in any coffee.

Now let's take two examples to better understand the nature of our roasted whole-bean coffee's density and how it relates to the brewing temperature. For your reference, a density reading of 4.000g/cl is quite common for high-quality, well-roasted coffee, and it equates to a 200°F water temperature.

First, let's take a very high-density coffee that is common with specialty roasters. This coffee is from Ethiopia, washed process, grown at 1,950 m.a.s.l., relatively uniform and small in size, and roasted in 10 minutes 30 seconds to 395°F, with only a minute of development after the start of first crack. This is a fairly fast roast with a relatively low finish temperature (don't forget that roasting probes differ greatly, so this is only low for some roasters), meaning it has not lost much moisture and the cell structure is likely still quite tightly packed. Its density reading is rather high at 4.423g/cl, which according to my chart indicates a brewing temperature of 204°F. The reason this coffee probably needs such a high temperature is that it has a) a lot of organic compounds, acids, and complex sugars; b) low to no roast/carbon characteristics; and c) tightly packed cells that will extract less easily.

Now let's go the other direction, to a low-density coffee that your typical specialty roaster may or may not buy. This coffee is from an undetermined origin, naturally processed, grown at 1,200 m.a.s.l., medium- to large-sized beans, and roasted in 13 minutes 15 seconds to 405°F, with 2 minutes of development after the start of first crack. This is an average coffee roast length and temperature, meaning the coffee has lost a decent amount of moisture and the cell structure has loosened up a bit. It also started with a less tightly packed cell structure because of the growing elevation and perhaps the varietal. The density reading is quite low, at 3.560g/cl, which means it should brew at 196°F. The reason this coffee probably needs such a low temperature is that it has a) a low amount of acids but a decent amount of sugars; b) identifiable roast/carbon characteristics; and c) loosely packed cells that are easy to extract fully.

Both of these coffees were specialty-grade in terms of defect count and cup score (85+), though the individual roaster's technique also had a role in the finished product. I know many roasters may avoid the second coffee because of its unknown origin or general cup profile, but when brewed with an appropriate temperature and technique, both were quite desirable.

These are just a couple of examples, but I believe the density-temperature correlation brings out the best in both of them. I suggest you play around with coffees of different densities using the handy chart in Figure 1— I think you'll be pleased with the result and will see the value in using whole-bean density to determine the water temperature of your brew. While the SCA's 195°F to 205°F ballpark range has given us a decent temperature window to refer to in the past, I think we can now improve our brews with more exact temperatures based on density.

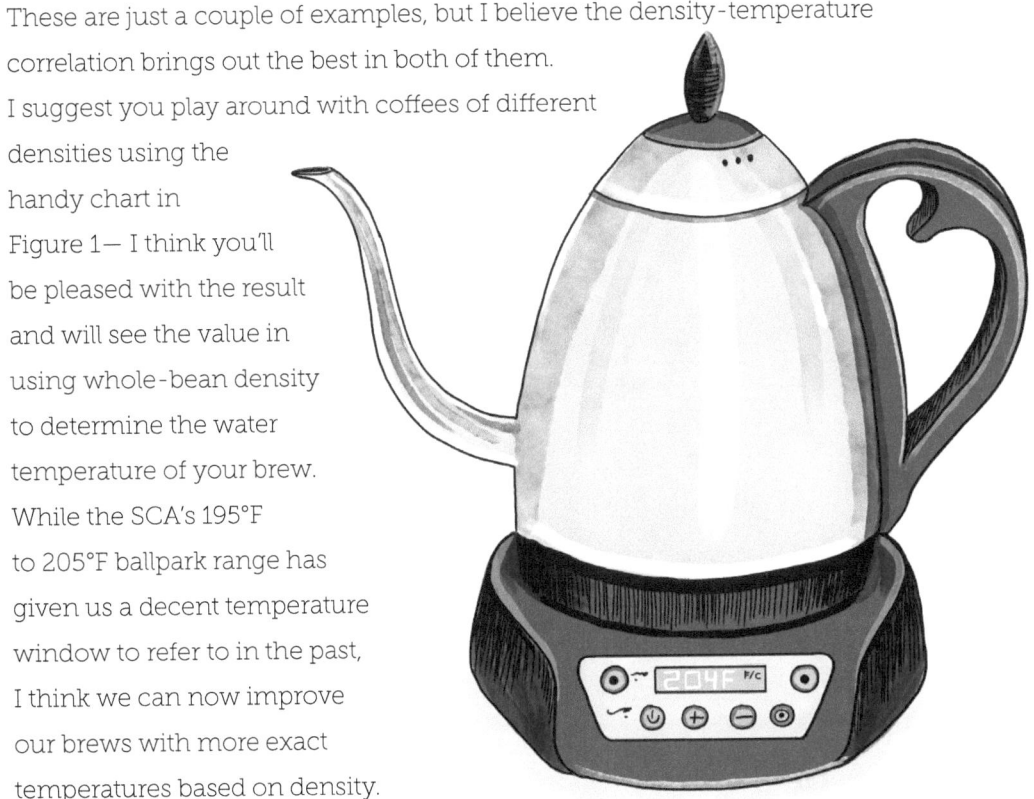

BREW FUNDAMENTAL TWO

DEVICE & FILTER

Around the mid-2000s, single-cup pour-over brewing became an unavoidable trend in the specialty-coffee realm. While it may no longer be the in-vogue brewing method it once was, pour-over is still the preferred choice of many specialty-coffee professionals—myself included.

What's become clear to me, in the last 12 years or so of making pour-over coffee regularly, is the immense amount of variability that exists in this realm. There are so many different devices—some that have existed for decades, others tried and true, and new ones popping up every year—that it can be hard to keep up, and my preferred devices have changed over the years.

I find myself drawn to drippers, and as one might expect, I'm most familiar with the more popular ones, such as the Kalita Wave, Hario V60, or AeroPress. These devices will of course produce different results in the cup, but in my years of using them, I've become specifically interested in how two factors—the devices' material and the filter paper used for brewing—impact the final result.

In this section, we'll dig into different pour-over brew devices' material and their filter options, and isolate some variables so that we can better understand how these factors impact extraction.

DEVICE MATERIAL

Most pour-over devices will be made from either ceramic, metal, plastic, or glass, and this material will undoubtedly influence the resulting cup. For example, with all brewing parameters equal, a thin metal dripper will produce a different result from a dripper made with twice as much metal, and both of those will almost certainly create a different flavor outcome than a coffee made with a standard ceramic dripper.

Interaction with heat

Before we look specifically at how various materials produce different results, let's first explore what's happening to brew device material during the brew process. Putting things into "elementary school science experiment" terms, when a cooler-temperature conductive material (like a coffee dripper) comes into contact with a warmer-temperature substance (like brewing water), the thermal energy is transferred to the cooler material until an equilibrium is reached (meaning they become the same temperature). So different coffee drippers will absorb, retain, or lose different amounts of thermal energy based on the material they're made from.

THE 3 MAIN PROPERTIES OF BREW MATERIALS

How the brew device material will react during brewing will depend largely on three main properties: conductivity, retention, and threshold.

Conductivity is how efficiently the device material moves heat from one point to another—like, say, from your brew slurry to the ambient air. Lower-conductivity material is generally more desirable, as it tends to draw heat away from the slurry more slowly, allowing the hot water to extract the coffee grinds more efficiently.

Retention refers to how well the material holds onto the heat it has captured, or has essentially stolen from your brew water. Low-retention material loses the heat it has stored extremely quickly, while high-retention material will continue to radiate heat for a long period after the heat source has been removed. Retention is very important with pour-over brews, as the higher the retention, the more efficient the extraction tends to be.

Threshold is essentially how hot the material can get during the brewing process. This temperature maximum is important because the hotter the material gets, the closer your slurry will get to equilibrium. For pour-over brews, low-threshold materials are preferred because they offer maximum brewing efficiency, with the material drawing less heat before reaching its threshold.

With these three properties in mind, let's dig into some brewing experiments I did using metal, plastic, and ceramic brewers to compare the specific impacts of brew material. (Note: Because I wanted to compare identical devices, I didn't do any tests using glass brewers, but I understand them to perform similar to metal brewers, with high conductivity, low to average retention, and a high threshold.)

Learning through experimentation

In these tests—shown in **Figures 4 and 5** on the next page—I used a Hario V60 brewer with metal (copper exterior), plastic, and ceramic cones. I brewed 10 batches for each material type, and all data was recorded to show trends in TDS, extraction yield, and more. The dose for

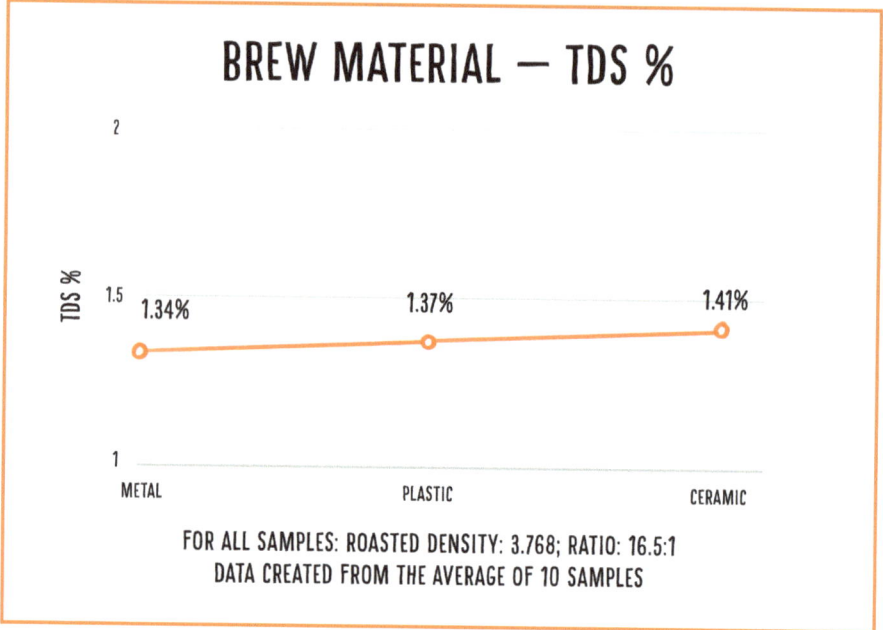

Figure 4

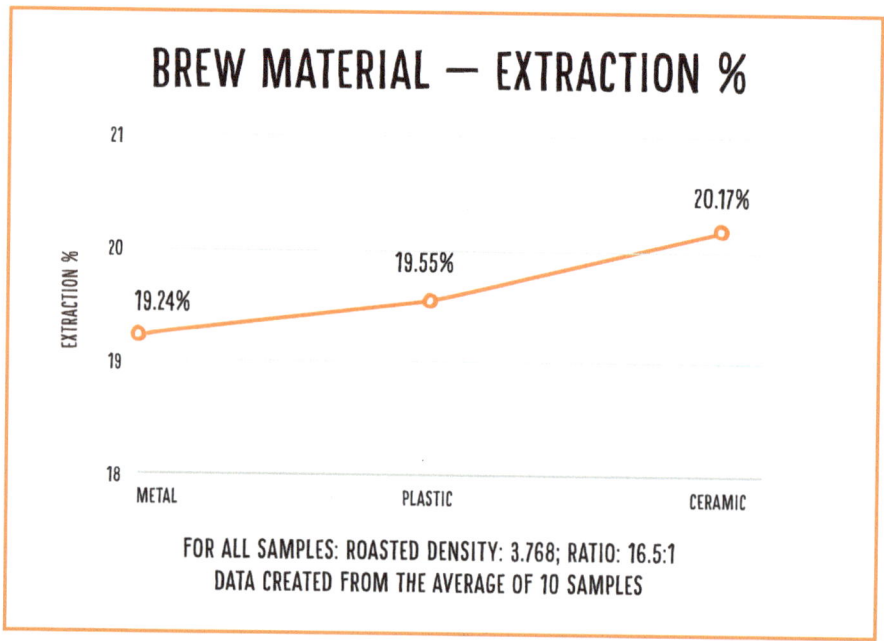

Figure 5

all samples was 18g (+/- .5g), the final beverage weight was 297g (or adjusted to maintain 1:16.5 brew ratio), the water TDS was 100-125 mg/l, the water temperature was 198°F, and the overall brew time was between 2 minutes 15 seconds and 2 minutes 30 seconds, with a 30-second bloom using 45g water. The pour was consistent, using concentric pouring until all grinds were saturated, then continuous center pouring to finish the brew weight. The coffee was ground on a Mahlkoenig Guatemala Lab grinder using the same setting for all samples.

Let's explore how these different materials behaved during our brew tests and affected our extraction numbers, starting with the metal brewer.

Metal

Right off the bat, the metal brewer had easily the lowest TDS and extraction yield of the three materials. This indicates that the metal brewer yielded the least palatable cup of coffee, and that is correct—I would describe the flavor of these brews as thin and sharp. The underlying sweetness of the coffee was lost, and the body was lacking. Looking at Figures 4 and 5, you can see that the TDS was on average 0.07% lower than the ceramic dripper, and the extraction was on average 0.93% lower. These numbers, while not enormous, are actually quite significant in terms of comparative brews—almost 1% in extraction yield is a huge flavor change.

A lower extraction can of course lead to these negative flavor results, but even when I adjusted my extraction numbers to match the ceramic dripper tests (by changing the grind setting and increasing the temperature of the brew water), the resulting coffee still had a less pleasing profile and sweetness. So even with a similar extraction, we didn't get the same flavor that the other materials produced. I believe this difference was due to the temperature variance from the exterior to the interior of the metal dripper.

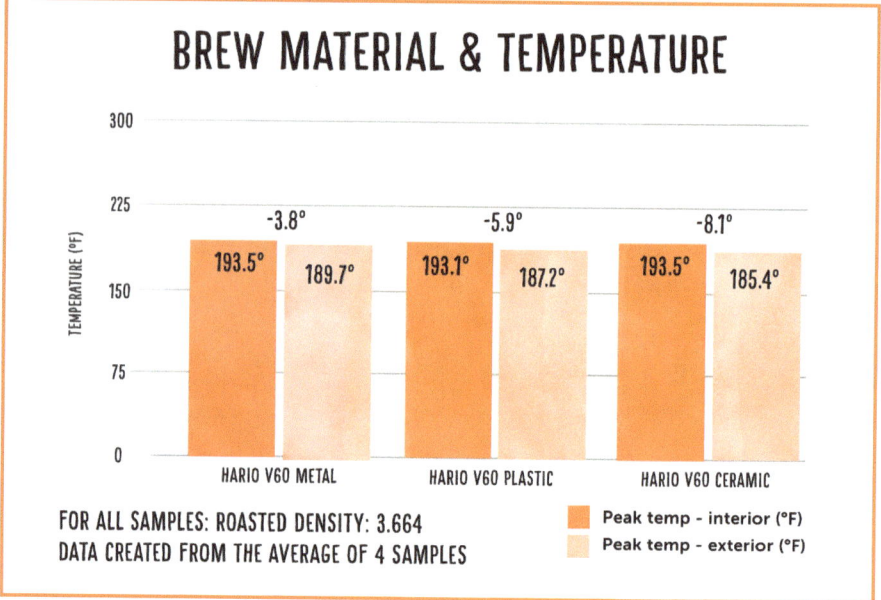

Figure 6

By measuring interior and exterior temperatures (see **Figure 6**), I found the metal dripper to have the most uniform temperature from interior to exterior, at only 3.8°F variance. The exterior was also significantly hotter than the other materials tested—2.7°F hotter than plastic and 4.3°F hotter than ceramic. As you might expect, that means that metal drippers get scalding hot during the brew process.

Metal behaves this way because it's an excellent conductor, actively pulling away heat from the slurry and distributing heat efficiently to the air in all directions. Though metal's very high threshold makes it get scalding during brewing, its retention is very low, meaning that the heat dissipates very quickly after the heat source (fresh hot water) is no longer added. This active heat loss lowered the efficiency at which we were brewing, resulting in our lower extraction yield numbers and the thin, sharp flavor in the cup.

Plastic

Moving on to the plastic dripper material, we saw a bit of a middle ground of TDS and extraction yield. Overall the average TDS was still 0.04% less than ceramic, and the extraction was on average 0.62% lower. Plastic clearly improved the

extractability of the coffee a bit compared to metal, but despite this increase, I still found the resulting brews to be one-dimensional and hollow, though the body was slightly improved over the metal dripper.

Once again, adjusting the extraction to match the ceramic dripper numbers did not result in an equally tasty cup. There was a general improvement, but the cup was missing complexity and depth. So let's look at the temperature variances on the plastic dripper to see what we can find to explain this observation.

The interior/exterior variance of plastic was higher than metal—a 5.9°F difference compared to 3.8°F—and while the exterior temperature was between metal and ceramic at 187.2°F, the interior temperature averaged 0.4°F lower than both.

So why does plastic behave this way? Plastic is a low-conductivity material, which as we've mentioned, is generally a good thing for our brews, as it draws heat away from the slurry less quickly. But in our tests, because of plastic's low retention and low conductivity, the heat disappeared and didn't radiate back into the slurry, which resulted in the one-dimensional taste in the cup. I found both the numbers and the taste in the cup produced by the plastic dripper intriguing—many in the specialty-coffee community find plastic superior to ceramic as a brew material due to its lower heat absorption, but I did not find this to be true.

Ceramic

Lastly, let's look at ceramic as a dripper material, which yielded the most desirable extraction numbers in our chart. A common assumption from the specialty-coffee community is that ceramic sucks the heat energy from the slurry, thus having a negative impact on the brew. While this phenomenon did occur somewhat,

as the heavy material required a good amount of heat energy to get up to temperature, it didn't result in a bad brew.

Let's look at the numbers again and remember the results that came with the ceramic dripper. It had the highest averages for TDS (1.41%) and extraction (20.17%). This was 0.03-0.06% higher in TDS and 0.62-0.93% higher in extraction yield than plastic and metal. So the extraction numbers were significantly higher for ceramic *despite* the fact that the heavy material obviously drew some of that heat energy away. This would seem to be further proof that once the ceramic material has absorbed its threshold, it then begins radiating heat back into the slurry and improving the extraction rate.

The flavor of these brews was consistently round, complex, highly sweet, and balanced. I believe the extraction numbers are in a good range for this to make sense, but what is making this happen?

After initially pulling heat from the slurry to hit the threshold, the retained heat in the ceramic material becomes highly efficient in the continued extraction. So in essence we are sacrificing a portion of the initial brew energy in order to fully insulate the brew slurry. In my tests I found the ceramic dripper's exterior temperature was on average 185.4°F from the middle to end of the brew, which was 1.8°F to 4.3°F lower than plastic and metal, and the ceramic dripper had the biggest temperature variance between interior and exterior at 8.1°F.

This interior/exterior temperature variance, though not completely logical, shows that an equilibrium temperature is not always necessary for a great brew. The ceramic material seems to prove an exception, due to the aforementioned insulation of the slurry (and potential radiant heat) improving the extraction rate. There is also the possibility of a slightly varied extraction from the exterior of the slurry to the interior, which could create some of the increased complexity that I tasted.

So to sum up the ceramic material, we have an average conductivity, meaning that it does draw heat but not incredibly quickly. It also has a relatively high threshold of heat, as it got very hot to the touch midway through the extraction. We also have a high retention of heat, possibly affected by the relatively slow conduction of that heat as well, but the amount of energy the dripper can hold is significant. The high retention is a large factor in the eventual thermal insulation of the slurry, which, as we saw in our tests, was of massive benefit in terms of our extraction.

Device material takeaways

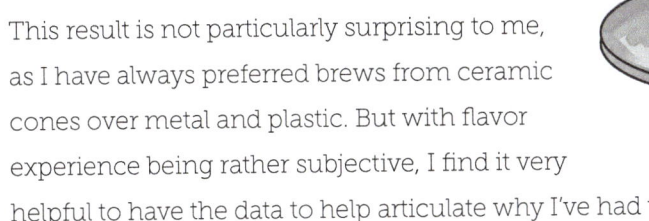

Due to its winning combination of conductivity, retention, and threshold, the ceramic dripper performed the best in these experiments—both in the numbers and in the cup—and proved to be the most efficient material, capable of delivering a high extraction quickly.

This result is not particularly surprising to me, as I have always preferred brews from ceramic cones over metal and plastic. But with flavor experience being rather subjective, I find it very helpful to have the data to help articulate why I've had this preference.

Following the parameters outlined at the beginning of this section, I hope you'll play around with brewing in different materials and measure your TDS and extraction numbers. Selecting the material of your brew device is a consequential decision that will undoubtedly influence the quality of your ultimate brew, and with a better understanding of how these materials impact extraction, we can ensure the best representation of the coffee we both consume and offer to the public.

FILTER PAPER

Aside from the material, another component of pour-over coffee devices that has fascinated me during my many years of making coffee is the effect of filter paper on extraction. The thickness and porosity of your filter paper—as well as the shape of the device—will have a distinct impact on the resulting cup. In this section, we'll play around with some different filters to better understand how they contribute to extraction, and look into how our choice of filter can yield the best results.

Filter versus shape

Paper filters will perform differently based on the shape of the dripper they're going into. Filters typically come crimped—or compressed into small folds—by the manufacturer, but the user will often need to maneuver them further for best results in the brew. Let's look at some of the main dripper shapes and how they impact filter use.

With **conical-shaped devices** like the Hario V60, the user typically folds the crimped side over to create a mostly smooth conical shape to go into the dripper. While this act of folding over the paper for cone-shaped drippers can seem unsightly, it has a relatively small impact on the resulting brew, as the folded section is minimal and the uniform shape of the filter creates a more even output from the slurry. (Sharp-eyed readers will note that the Chemex is a conical-shaped brewer that doesn't follow the folding pattern detailed here—with the Chemex, you end up with a triple layer on one half of the cone and a single layer on the other. While this is an exception to the rule for this brewer shape, the Chemex is still a conical-shaped brew device.)

With **truncated-cone drippers** like the Melitta 1-hole or Clever coffee dripper, the necessary folding of the filter paper does impact the brew. Filters for this dripper design must be folded on the side and bottom along the crimped paper in order to create a level coffee bed, and folding the crimp under the filter forms a barrier for the extracted liquid to escape the holes at the bottom of the dripper. The extra resistance this creates can slow down the overall brew, but that isn't necessarily a bad thing— that will depend on the other factors happening in the brew. Because the flow of liquid is naturally slower with this dripper shape, a coarser grind is usually used to produce the best results, as a finer grind can lead to over-extracted flavors.

With **flat-bottomed drippers** such as the Kalita Wave, the filter's ridges will help keep the filter stable in its more vertical position; this commonly leads to grinds getting caught in the ridges in this dripper design, which can impact extraction. However, this is somewhat countered by flat-bottomed drippers having the largest amount of surface area in contact with the slurry itself, due to their wider bottom as well as the increased surface offered by the ridges themselves. So while some

DEVICE & FILTER SHAPES

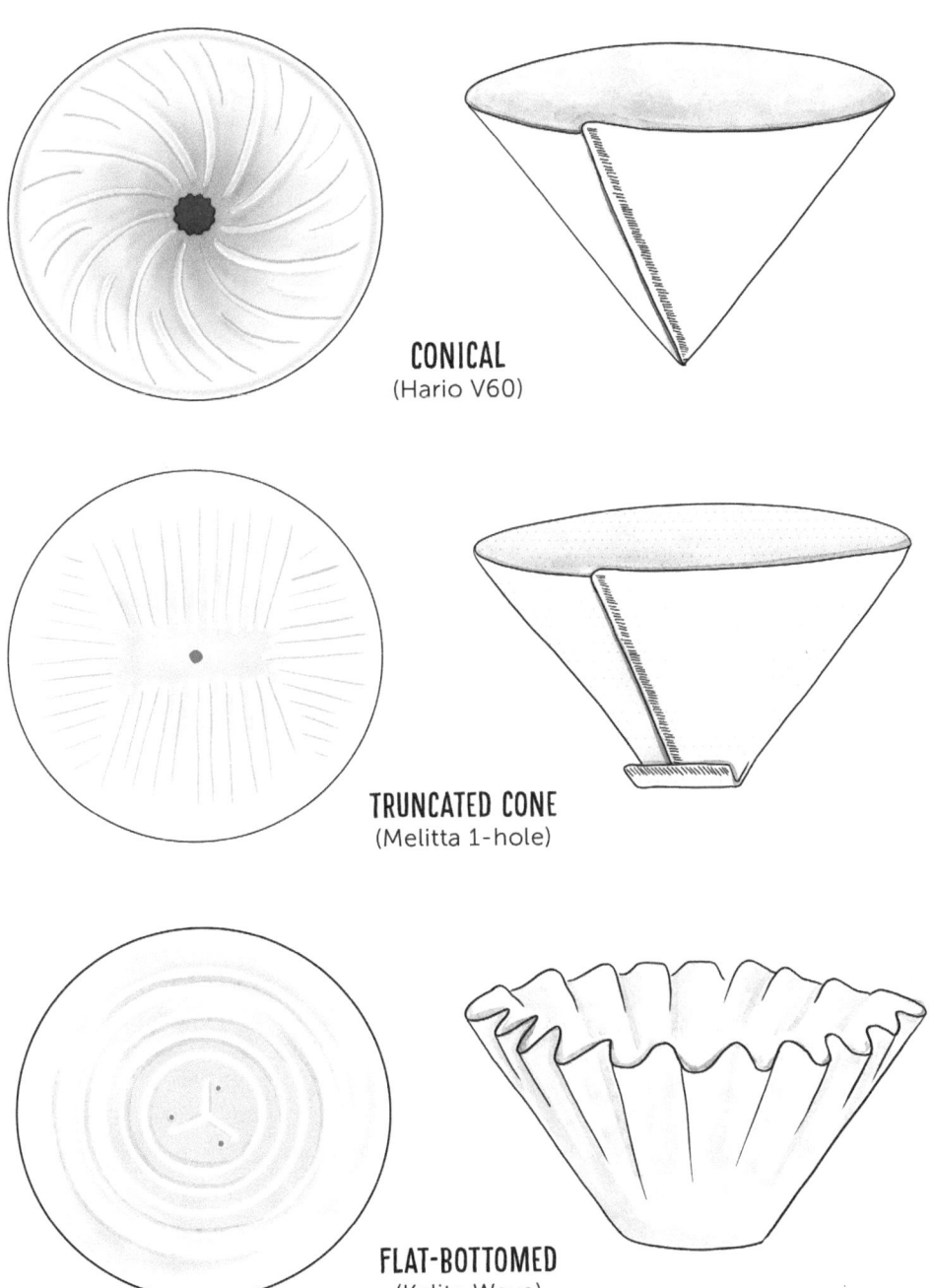

CONICAL
(Hario V60)

TRUNCATED CONE
(Melitta 1-hole)

FLAT-BOTTOMED
(Kalita Wave)

grinds can get caught in the filter paper, the extra surface area mitigates clogging from fine grinds, which can outweigh this inconvenience.

The dripper shape will influence how the filter performs during extraction; another important factor on this performance is the makeup of the filter, which we'll explore now.

WHAT'S YOUR ANGLE?

One factor influencing how a paper filter fits into your coffee dripper is the angle of the dripper's walls—a feature sometimes reflected in the dripper's name. For example, the "60" in the Hario V60 refers to the angle in degrees of the dripper's shape. A higher number toward 90 will indicate a steeper slope—for example, as seen in Saint Anthony Industries' C70 brewer—and a lower number indicates a more relaxed slope. The slope will impact how stacked or even the grinds will be in the dripper, and will also dictate the overall surface area that your filter will cover when it's in the dripper.

Understanding what's in our filters

There are of course a vast assortment of paper filters available on the market, and it can be difficult to know which filter is right for your brew device. I've found that in evaluating paper filters, it's most helpful to look at two main characteristics: **porosity** and **thickness**. Porosity refers to how big and frequent the gaps are between the filter's paper fibers, while thickness indicates the distance between the filter's opposing sides. These two factors have a considerable impact on the end brew.

You've probably noticed the thickness of different brewers' paper filters just by handling them. Some filters, like the V60 or AeroPress, are quite thin and light, while others, like Chemex or Kalita Wave filters, tend to be very thick and heavy. Porosity is a little harder to spot at a quick glance, but if you look closely at the filters, you can usually see some indication of the size and number of holes in the paper. The Kalita Wave filter, for example, is less porous, while the Melitta

COMMON FILTERS, MAGNIFIED

MELITTA TRUNCATED CONE

Filter with no magnification

Magnification 0.8x: inside

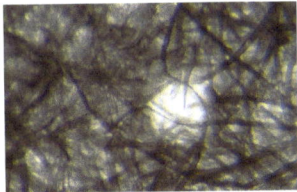
Magnification 6.4x: inside

HARIO V60

Filter with no magnification

Magnification 0.8x: inside

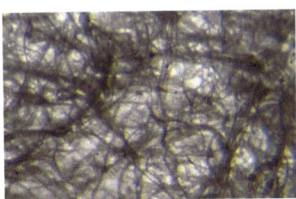
Magnification 6.4x: inside

AEROPRESS

Filter with no magnification

Magnification 0.8x: inside

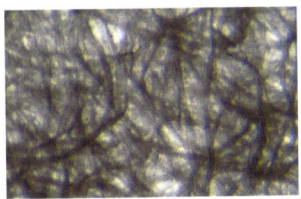
Magnification 6.4x: inside

KALITA WAVE

Filter with no magnification

Magnification 0.8x: inside

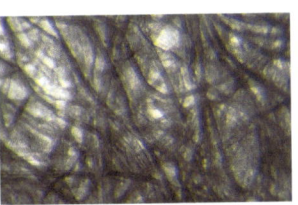
Magnification 6.4x: inside

CHEMEX

Filter with no magnification

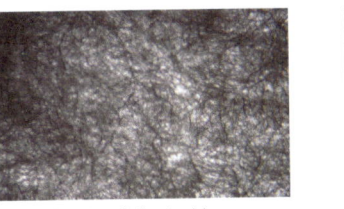
Magnification 0.8x: inside

Magnification 6.4x: inside

Brew Fundamental 2: DEVICE & FILTER

truncated-cone filter has many large holes punched in it, making it more porous. (Check out the magnified photos of coffee filters on the previous page for a closer look—thanks to the lovely guys at Third Wave Water for these photos!)

The thickness and porosity of your filter will affect both the look and taste of the resulting brew based on the amount of liquid and particles that are let through. Thicker filters—in which the paper fibers are more heavily "stacked" in layers—will trap more solids to result in a clearer brew, but this can come at the cost of less articulate flavors, as the coffee is extracted more slowly. Thinner filters will create a stronger brew because dissolved solids tend to come through more easily. And while a thinner filter may lead to a slightly cloudier coffee, this shouldn't be too much of a concern, as most commercial paper filters—even thin ones—will not allow large settleable solids into the brew.

Porosity operates a little differently: More porous filters typically lead to a cloudier brew, as larger particles permeate the paper, but they also often produce a flavor profile that is more muddled and sometimes sour. Less porous filters will lead to a clearer brew because fewer particles make it through, and they will generally extract better.

However, this scenario gets slightly more convoluted when you factor in that thickness and porosity are not mutually exclusive. A filter may very well be thin to the touch but have a very fine porosity, while conversely some filters may be quite thick but with larger pores. In these cases, the filters may behave in contradictory ways from what I described in the previous paragraphs. But as you pay closer attention to the thickness and porosity of paper filters, you will likely notice if one of these characteristics is more dominant in a given filter, and can adjust your brewing accordingly.

46 How to Get the Best from Your Coffee

Putting filters to the test

As I've come to understand how filters' thickness and porosity change the brew, I have started to wonder specifically how applying different filters to the same brew device impacts extraction. I decided to further explore this by conducting an experiment using the manufacturer-recommended filters from several well-known brew devices: AeroPress, Melitta 1-hole dripper, Chemex, Hario V60, and Kalita Wave. I cut each filter to the size of an AeroPress disc filter and brewed coffee on an AeroPress. The results were eye-opening for me, and I think they explain a lot about why we see different outcomes with various brew devices and their standard filters (see **Figures 7-10** on the next page).

The resultant liquid from different filters was significantly impacted by the type of filter, as evidenced both in the charts and in the flavor I evaluated in the cup. The best-tasting brews were also the best extracted based on the numbers—see V60 and AeroPress in Figure 9. I chalk up these positive results in large part to these filters being thin and light. That isn't so much to say that thinner filter paper is always superior, but I do believe it is more efficient at extracting coffee liquid that is more intense and flavorful.

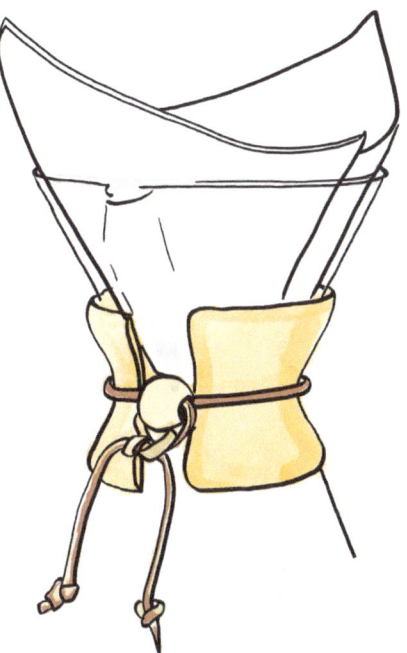

On the other side of the spectrum, the least-balanced brews had two of the worst extractions—see the Kalita Wave and Chemex in Figures 9 and 10. If you are like me, you've tasted many delicious brews from both Kalita Wave and Chemex devices before. So why didn't their filters lead to tasty brews on the AeroPress? It appears that the thicker paper in these filters lowered the extraction yield in terms of what is in the cup, as seen in the low extraction numbers. As mentioned, this happens largely because the thicker the paper, the more fibers used, and thus the higher chance that the filter will retain larger particles and let fewer dissolved solids into the final brew.

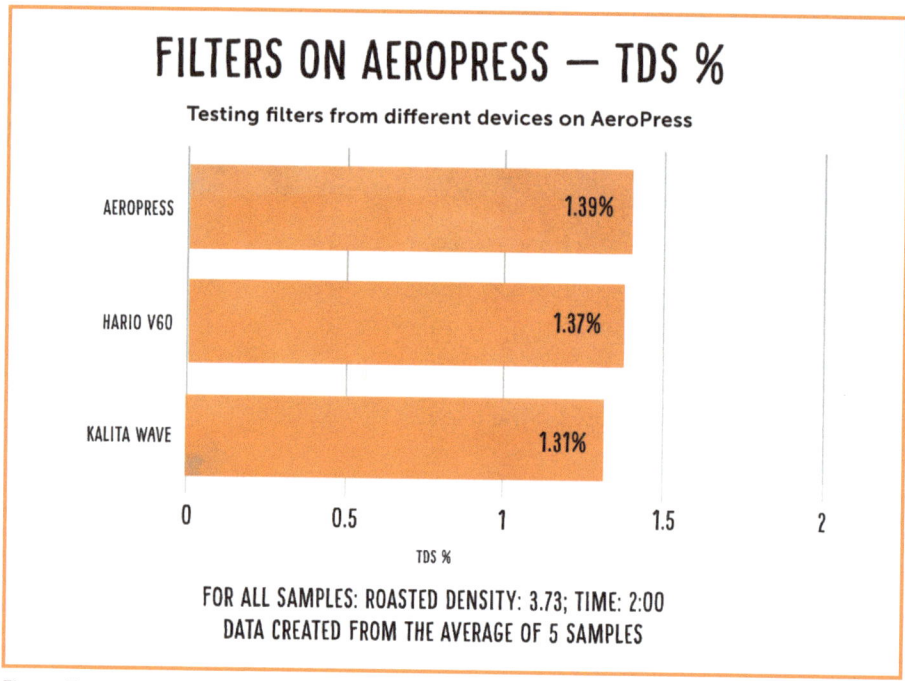

Figure 7

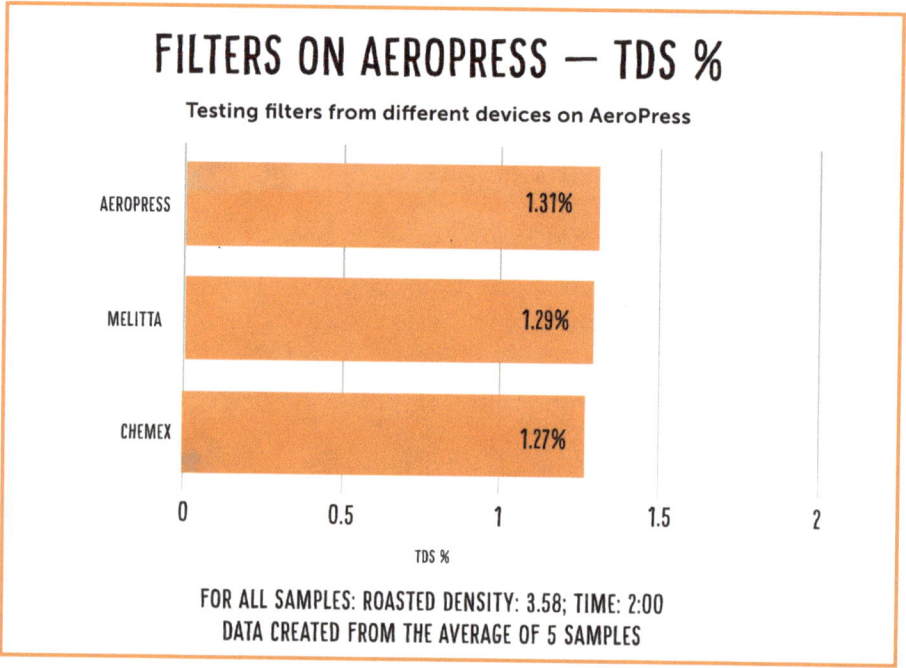

Figure 8

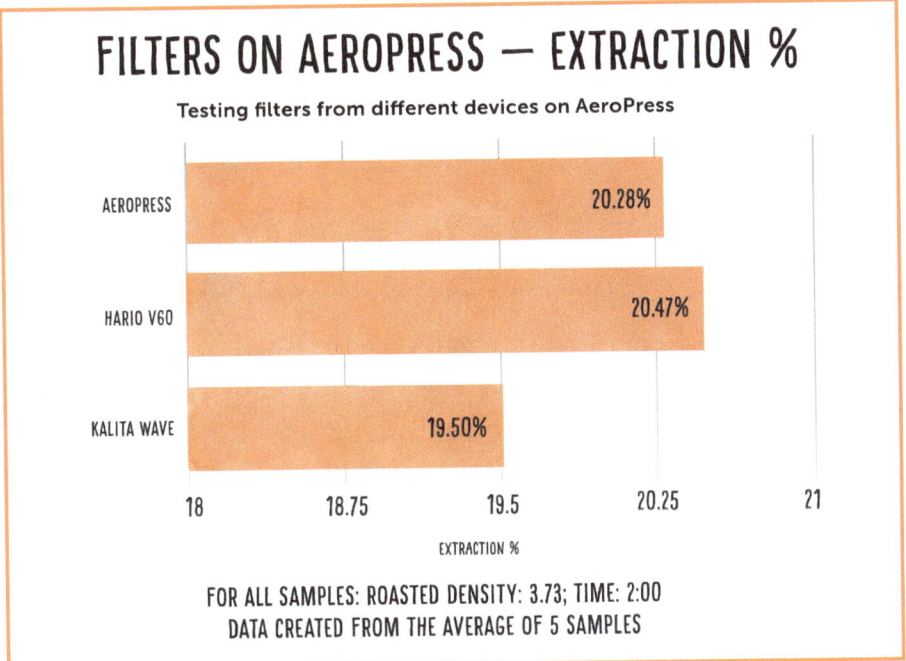

Figure 9

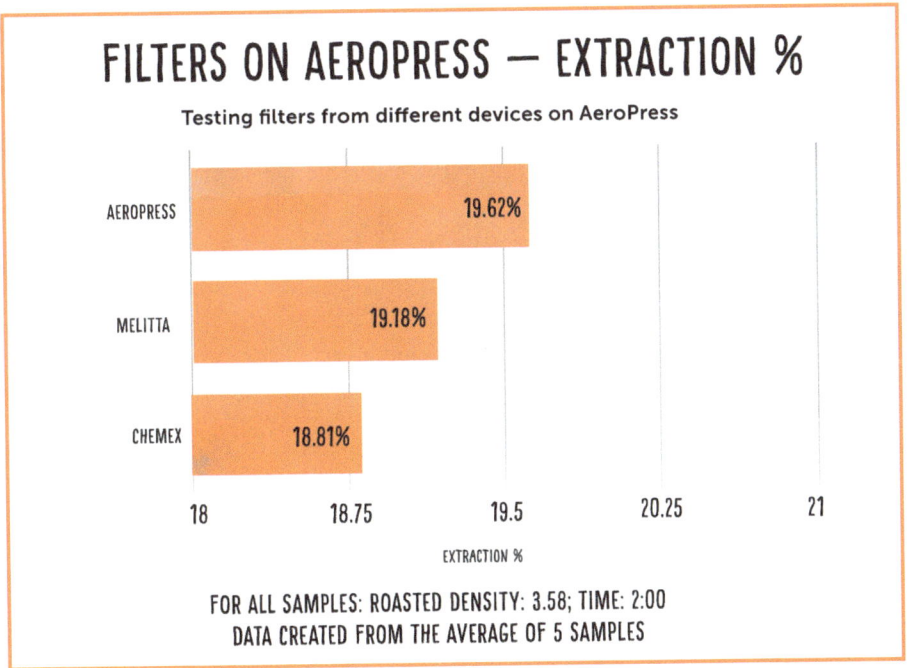

Figure 10

Melitta truncated-cone filter

Chemex filter

Kalita Wave filter

The tests also showed a correlation between the extraction percentages and the TDS levels of the brews, as seen in Figures 7 and 8. In general, the better-extracted brews were also stronger (i.e., had higher TDS percentages), though the range of TDS readings was significantly more narrow than the extraction readings.

I observed a couple more tidbits from the experiment that I think are noteworthy. One is that the Melitta truncated cone that was tested yielded wildly inconsistent brews, both in numbers and in flavor. As mentioned, this particular filter, which is commonly sold, has a series of large holes punched throughout, which makes the filter more porous, and thus leads to more inconsistency as different amounts of liquid and dissolved solids make it through during any given brew. These large holes may not be present in every Melitta truncated-cone filter, but this particular style is quite commonly found in retailers around the United States.

Two, the unpalatable results with the Chemex filter reminded me that this filter is prone to clogging very easily—even when tested in a different device like the AeroPress—because its thickness is slow to let brewed coffee through. Based on these numbers, I think that to get an appropriate brew strength with the Chemex filter, you must either grind finer or increase your dose. However, both of these actions will also increase the amount of fine particles in the slurry, which will once again clog the paper filter. So if you have issues with Chemex brews clogging, it may simply be the nature of the filter paper causing multiple issues that are difficult to avoid.

Filter takeaways

I am not too surprised that the Hario V60 filters yielded some of my favorite results in the filter tests on AeroPress, as these filters are a regular element in my preferred brewing routine with the Hario V60. They have small pores but are rather thin, which allows for a more efficient extraction and a clean, strong cup.

Overall, these tests yielded not just intriguing results, but a reminder that playing around with different filters is a fun avenue for flavor discovery. Yes, it's fairly unconventional to mix and match filters and drippers. This is because brewing equipment manufacturers typically design their devices in a way that necessitates (or at least highly suggests) using their proprietary filters.

However, I believe these suggested parameters can be overcome; even though there is a limitation to what shape may fit into which brew device, we can in fact use different filters with a little creativity. Cutting and folding in various ways can help you discover new versions of a brewer you thought you knew. You can easily use a cone-shaped filter in a truncated cone dripper simply by folding the bottom of the cone up. Flat-bottom filters can be refolded into a cone shape if desired. You can even make a flat-bottomed filter of sorts by inverting the bottom of a cone-shaped filter (turning the bottom portion inside out), creating a circular ring of space that fits right into that flat-bottomed dripper. These options are fun to experiment with, and though they will change some basic structure of how the coffee brews, the biggest impact will come from the porosity and thickness of the filters themselves.

I do hope you'll try some of these experiments on your own; you may find that the best brew you've ever tasted is the result of one of these hybridizations that you never would have discovered otherwise!

BREW FUNDAMENTAL THREE

GRINDING

The grinding of coffee—and its subsequent size and shape—has been a frequently discussed topic in the specialty-coffee sphere for the past several years, with many people holding strong opinions about the "best" way to grind to produce a great-tasting brew.

Like many of the subjects we obsess about in coffee, grinding is fairly complicated, largely due to the nature of how we grind coffee. During the grinding process, whole-roasted coffee beans are cut multiple times to create an average particle of the desired size. Inevitably, due to the inexactness of even the most advanced grinders, not every coffee particle ends up being exactly the same size, and this leads to an endless amount of complex scenarios for coffee pros to obsess about.

In this section, we'll explore an important concept in coffee grinding: the effect of particle size on brew flavor. Namely, we'll look at uniformity, the phenomenon in which ground coffee particles are of a similar size, and compare it to the results of varied particle sizes in our grind. First we'll discuss some theory around uniformity and varied particle sizes, then we'll jump into experiments that put these ideas to the test.

But before we tackle these topics, let's again put on our science hat for a moment to look at what is happening from a chemistry perspective between our ground coffee and our water as we brew.

Solvent, solutes, and solution

In basic chemistry terms, a cup of brewed coffee is a solution of extracted coffee particles and water. By definition, a solution is a mixture composed of one or more solutes (dissolvable particles) and a solvent (a substance that dissolves a soluble, which is a compound that will potentially extract). Because water is the only solvent typically used in the creation of the solution known as brewed coffee, and we have found our consistent and reliable water source in Fundamental 1, that will be our solvent for this book. So we have our solvent and we know what solution we are making (brewed coffee); let's focus on the solubles in particular—which in our case will be found in ground coffee. (And a quick terminology note: I will mostly use the term "solubles" rather than "solutes" to refer to the undissolved particles going forward. The terms are quite similar—see the Glossary for exact definitions—but the former is typically more accurate for what we're discussing with ground coffee.)

The roasted coffee bean holds within its cells numerous particles that are either solubles or insolubles (such as plant cellulose, proteins, or fats). The consensus is that solubles account for about 30-35% of the coffee bean composition, so about one-third of a roasted coffee bean can be dissolved if we try hard enough. However, the commonly preferred flavor components tend to constitute only around 18-21% of the extraction—which is a rather small window of extraction to hit! What I find important to note is that the desirable flavors that make up a delicious cup of coffee are not simply determined by the overall dissolved amount of solutes. Instead, our best cups of coffee tend to be determined by the ability to extract the positive flavor solubles with a minimal amount of the negative ones. The necessity of extracting the positive solubles is why we must focus on all the different aspects of the brewing process presented in this book.

From the purely physical standpoint of how to get those positive solubles in the cup, when our solvent water is added to freshly ground coffee, an initial reaction takes place in which various gasses are expelled from the grinds. When this happens, water's ability to extract the majority of solubles is significantly diminished. This is why we typically bloom the grinds in a pour-over brew; as a small amount of water soaks into the grinds during the bloom, the coffee's gasses are mostly expelled. Then when we return to pouring the water, the solubles are much more quickly and efficiently pulled into the solution—and as long as we have used the proper methods, we will be capable of getting a great flavor in that extraction.

USING THE TRUSTY SIEVE

Grinding coffee is a rather complex subject, and I want to acknowledge that there are many deeper levels we can explore to better understand this art, including using tools like laser diffraction testing and conducting advanced calculations of the grinds' surface area. But in the spirit of accessibility, I used simple sieving and weighing for the tests in this section to get a snapshot of grinders' output range.

GRIND UNIFORMITY VERSUS VARIED PARTICLE SIZES

As the brief chemistry synopsis shows, the solubles of ground coffee are delicate entities, and it takes skill and knowledge to turn them into a flavorful brew, including knowing which size of grind particles will produce the best results.

But before we go any further on the topic, let's better define grind particle sizes and how we measure them—this is typically done by the micron (μm). A micron is one-thousandth of a millimeter in length, or one-millionth of a meter. For coffee grinds, this refers to the smallest diameter of a given coffee particle, and that is most easily determined by the size of sieve hole it will fit through.

For filter brewing, most particles in a given grind will fall between 300μm and 1,400μm, though there will be some grinds above and below that range. Coffee particles larger than 1,400μm are typically considered to be "boulders," and are recognizable for being noticeably bigger than the other grinds. For the testing in this book, coffee particles smaller than 300μm are considered "fine dust," and these teensy grinds are a natural byproduct of the grinding process—similar to how cutting wood generates sawdust. Fine dust is a somewhat controversial topic in the grinding realm, so we'll be returning to it shortly.

But back to defining our terms when it comes to particle sizes. As one might expect, when we talk about **uniform grind size**, we are referring to all particles in our grind being of a similar measurement in the above range—let's say 500-800μm. And when we discuss **varied particle sizes**, we're talking about our grind featuring particles of that entire range, including fine dust and boulders.

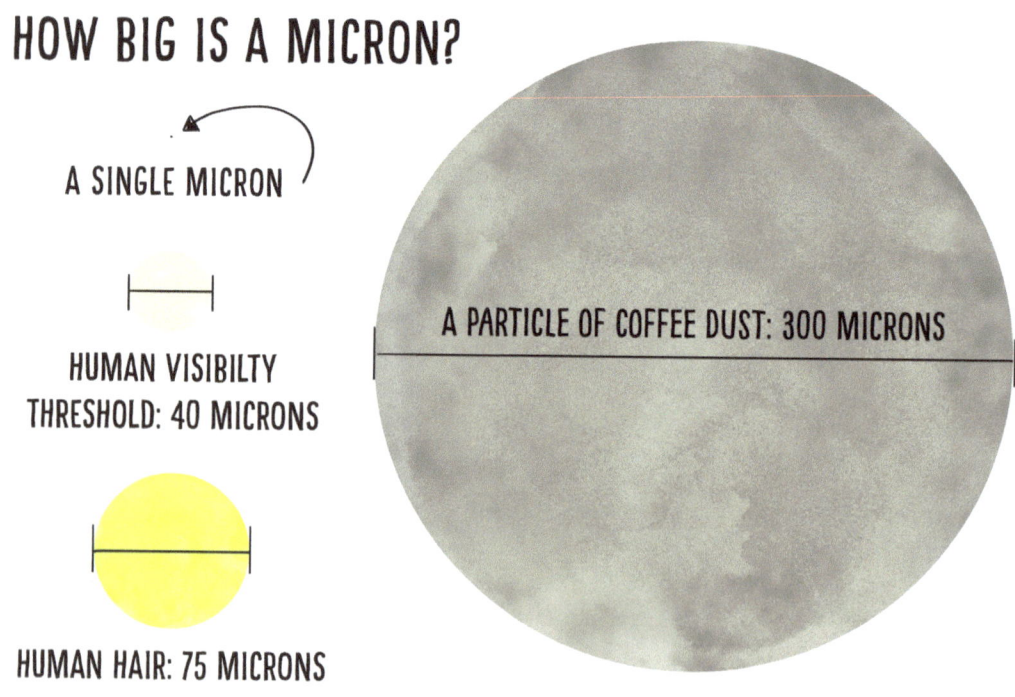

HOW BIG IS A MICRON?

A SINGLE MICRON

HUMAN VISIBILTY THRESHOLD: 40 MICRONS

HUMAN HAIR: 75 MICRONS

A PARTICLE OF COFFEE DUST: 300 MICRONS

As our specialty-coffee world has evolved, we have changed our expectations of what should be in a given grind. Even 15 years ago, we would typically see a broad range of particles in our ground coffee—typically in that 300-1,400µm range, with the small amount of outliers on each side. When hot water was poured over these grinds, great-tasting coffee could be made. What we had a hard time doing was recreating an amazing brew *consistently*.

Our relationship with consistency has changed over the years as we've improved our methods behind the bar. We are now more precise in measuring coffee (both in dose and grind size), and this intentionality has led us to a deeper understanding of how a specific grinder—and grind size—may influence our brews. This change has led many specialty-coffee professionals to start preferring that the grinds in their brews be completely uniform.

Many people in this contingent approach coffee extraction from the view that mathematically speaking, completely uniform grinds will extract at an even rate, which will yield higher extractions. This school of thought believes that uniformity will lead to more "correct" results in the cup—or, in other words, a true representation of a particular coffee. However, those on the other side of the debate will tell you that a range of sizes, including fine dust in small amounts, is an important component in bringing out the best of your filter brew.

While I believe both perspectives have merit, I do find myself preferring one approach to grind sizes over the other. **Because different particle sizes extract at different rates, I believe that having a variety of particle sizes in our brew is necessary to creating a great flavor with complexity and a desirable body.** There is a lot to unpack with this statement, so to help illustrate these different performances in the cup—and to explain why my preference falls where it does— let's turn to some tests putting grind sizes into action.

Testing particle size theory

The first set of tests I conducted used two different grinders to explore their grind profiles and see what we could learn from their particle size breakdown and the flavor of the resulting brew.

WHAT DO VARIOUS GRIND SIZES LOOK LIKE?

Less than 300μm

300-500μm

500-800μm

800-1,000μm

1,000-1,400μm

For these tests, I decided to use the EK43 and Guatemala Lab grinders by Mahlkoenig. This company in particular has been gaining a huge amount of attention in the specialty-coffee realm, and their grinders are considered by some to be the current standard.

Despite the EK43 and Guatemala Lab being manufactured by the same company and having very similar functions, their grind output is significantly different. This happens in large part because of their different burr sizes: The EK43 uses 98mm flat burrs in a vertical orientation, while the Guatemala Lab grinder has 71mm flat burrs, also arranged vertically.

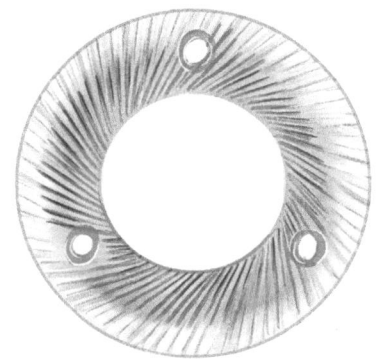
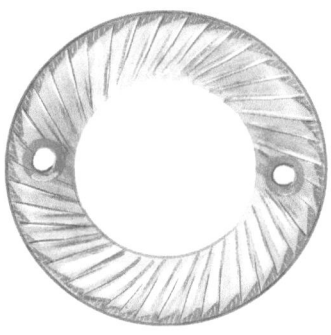

EK43: 98MM BURRS   GUATEMALA LAB: 71MM BURRS

Analyzing particle size

With our grinders set, I conducted the tests by grinding our coffee—a Kenya Ruthagati AA—to a standard (medium-fine) extraction for a Hario V60. I then used my sieve to measure the resulting grind sizes—we can look at Figure 11 on the next page for a visual representation of what I found, measuring the weight in grams of each resulting grind size range. I could have broken these sizes into even smaller separations, but the groups shown here are a good representation of where major extraction impacts come from. The big spike of one size for the EK43 indicates its more uniform median particle size, while the boxy hill shape of the Guatemala Lab grinds shows us its bigger range of particle sizes.

Looking at these grinders, we can tie the results at least in part to their aforementioned burr sizes. The EK43 made a more precise (i.e., uniform) grind by

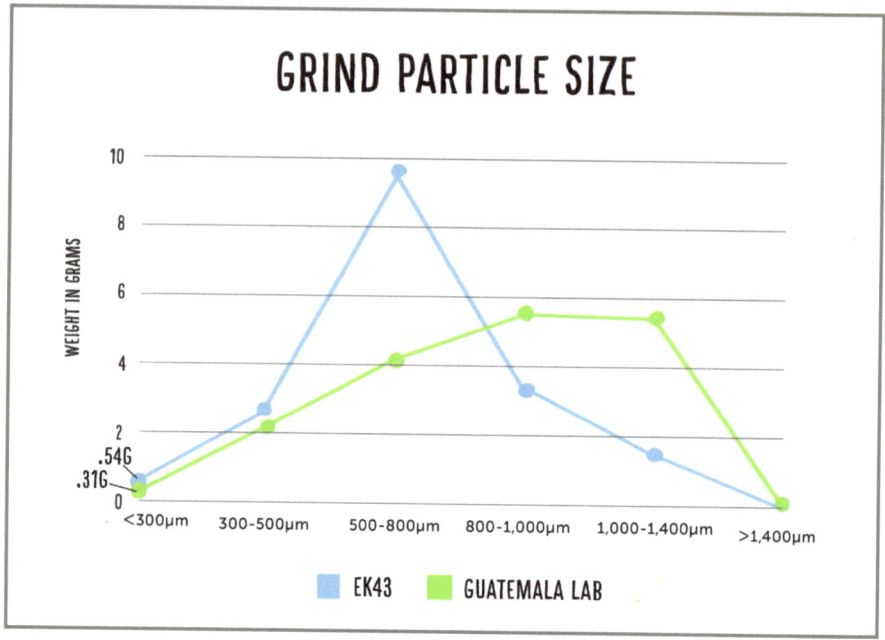

Figure 11

cutting the bigger particles down as they moved across the larger burr set, while also creating more fine particles in the dose. On the other hand, the Guatemala Lab made a bit less precise of a grind profile, in part because of the smaller burr size—with less grinding surface area for the coffee particles to pass through, there is less time for cutting of the grinds and thus less uniformity. There were a few larger boulders (grinds above 1,400μm) on the Guatemala Lab, but there were also fewer fine particles.

As mentioned, the chart in Figure 11 was designed using weight as the measurement for each grind size; however, I think that looking at the data only in this way can obscure important understandings of the grind profile. Another way to look at these grind profiles is to calculate them as a percentage of the overall dose weight (see **Figures 12-13**). In these charts, we see the breakdown of each grind size range for the EK43 and Guatemala Lab grinders, respectively.

Looking at Figures 12 and 13, the most obvious thing to note is that the EK43 had a higher percentage of grind sizes from 800μm and lower compared to the Guatemala Lab. In Figure 12, we can see that 500-800μm was clearly the primary grind size for the EK43, and we had an increase in the 300-500μm amount by

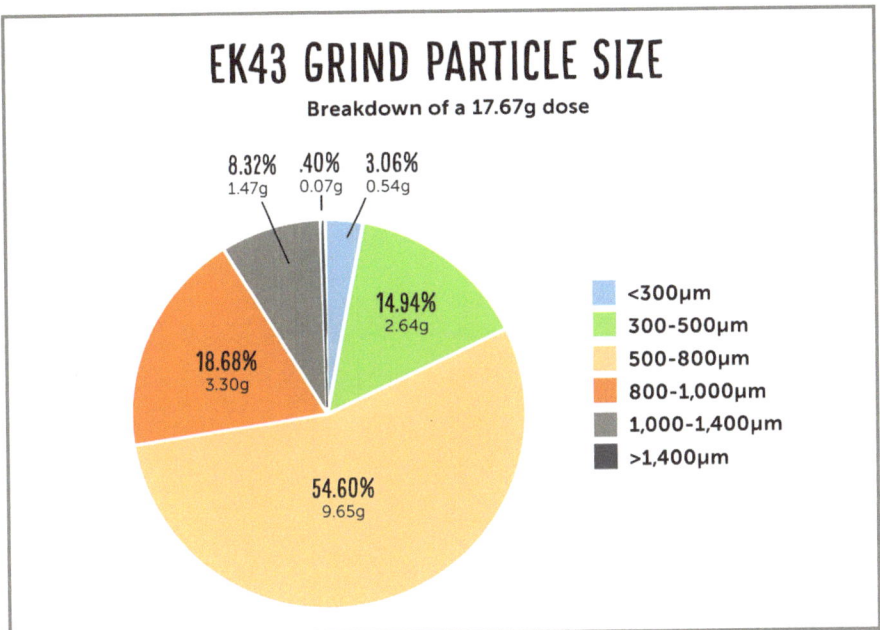

Figure 12

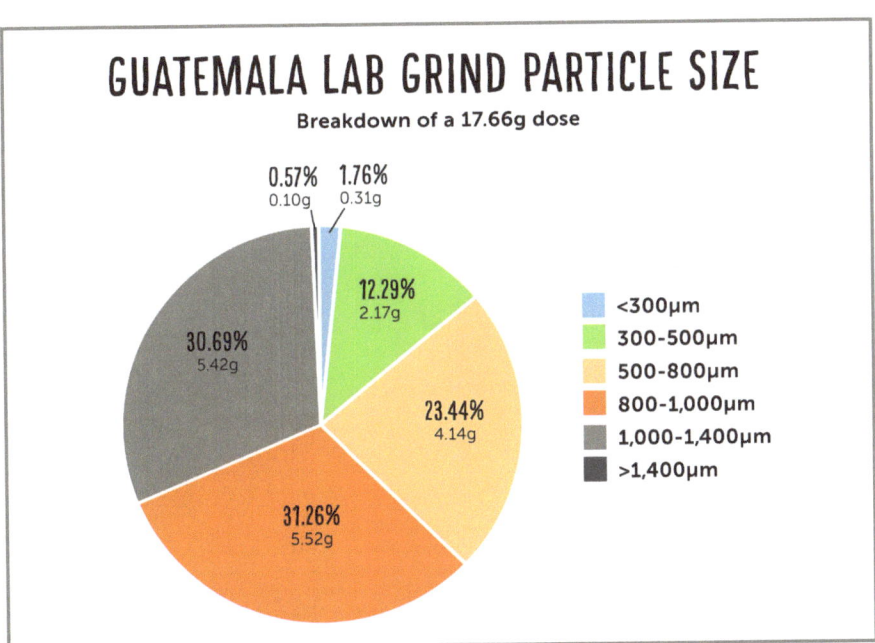

Figure 13

0.47g compared to the Guatemala Lab, and <300μm by 0.23g, which are not insignificant amounts! The Guatemala Lab grinder, as seen in Figure 13, had the lower numbers on the fine side and increased numbers on the higher grind sizes. While the 500-800μm grind size was over 30% lower for the Guatemala Lab grinder, the 800-1,000μm size increased by 12.66%, and the 1,000-1,400μm size increased by a whopping 22.37%!

Seeing this data in pie chart form in these figures, it's clear that we have a dominant—or uniform!—grind size with the EK43, and a true variety of particle sizes with the Guatemala Lab.

Assessing the flavor

Now that we know that the EK43 produced a more uniform grind and the Guatemala Lab yielded a varied profile of particle sizes, let's turn to how these coffees performed in the cup. I brewed both grinders' coffee in a Hario V60, finishing draw-down for both at 2 minutes 30 seconds.

In the resulting cups, the brew made from the EK43 grinder's coffee had a slightly higher extraction yield at 20.9% versus 20.4% for the Guatemala Lab brew. Now, by the modern perception that uniformity leads to higher extraction, the Guatemala Lab brew should have been nowhere close to the EK43 in terms of extraction yield, yet it was actually quite close.

In the flavor department, the EK43 brew had a very clear acidity, a strong flavor of grapefruit (without the sweetness), relatively light body, and slight dryness, which indicated the coffee was over-extracted a bit. I would say the flavor was easy to identify but not a highly satisfying cup. On the other side, the Guatemala Lab brew had a lower intensity of acid, which was more rounded and balanced with the other flavor components. The body was of a medium weight, and a distinct sweetness was present. Little bitterness or dryness indicated that this was a very good extraction by taste.

Connecting particle size to flavor

Here's where things get really fun (for a coffee nerd at least!), as we can now ask and answer the question: Why did the grinders' respective grind profiles produce these results in the cup?

To put it simply, different coffee particles extract at different rates, with smaller particles extracting faster than larger ones. I've known this to be true from observation, but I gathered my own data (see **Figure 14** on the next page) to see how specific grind sizes extract independently. To do this, I sieved the grinds and extracted each grind size separately, to the same proportion of a standard brew (1:16.5). I then measured the amount that each one was extracting into the brew.

The results were not too surprising in that the smaller particles yielded more solutes and the larger particles yielded fewer, though there was one particularly odd exception: The <300μm grinds extracted less efficiently than the 300-500μm particles. We can ponder why this might be; my theory is that the amount of fines and water was simply too low to be measured this way. But it's accurate to say that as the grind size got smaller, the strength and yield tended to increase. When we understand this trend based on the data, we can begin correlating everything that we have learned a bit better.

So in the brew from the EK43, we had a larger concentration of smaller particle sizes—including a higher amount of fine dust—which extracted faster and led to

GRIND SIZE BREAKDOWN

13.44g Individual Grind Extractions	TDS %	Extraction %
<300µm	1.38%	20.30%
300-500µm	1.48%	22.15%
500-800µm	1.21%	17.28%
800-1,000µm	1.03%	15.42%
1,000-1,400µm	0.86%	12.69%

Figure 14

the dryness that indicated an over-extracted cup. However, we also had a very obvious acidity and specific flavors, which we can correlate to the high uniformity seen in the peak of EK43 particles in Figure 11, as this concentration of one particular characteristic of the coffee is a common trait of uniformly ground coffee.

On the other hand, the larger average particle size from the Guatemala Lab grinder, and the lower amount of fines in particular, explains why it was less likely to taste over-extracted. There were also a significant amount of positive flavors and textures coming from the Guatemala Lab grinder, which simply must be coming from the interaction of a mixed extraction rate (i.e., different particles extracting at different times).

As Ted Lingle tells us in *The Coffee Brewing Handbook*, the fastest-extracting compounds—which often come from the smallest particle sizes—tend to be organic acids, caramelized sugars, caffeine, and salts. With a healthy representation of these compounds, as well as a reasonable amount of the other, slower-extracting solubles (fatty acids, sucrose, and phenols) in the brew, we were able to achieve a complex, tasty brew like the one made from the Guatemala Lab's coffee.

Grind size takeaways

While the debate on grind particle size continues to carry on and evolve in our industry, I clearly come down on one side. For my palate, brews made from varied particle sizes taste better in general, with a more pleasing body, quality of acidity, and overall balance.

To me, embracing varied particle sizes is in some ways embracing what current grinding technology is giving us. In modern grinding, there is no way to grind coffee without making fine dust. If a barista wants to eliminate fine dust and create a totally uniform grind, that will entail jumping through extra hoops. Using fine dust in small amounts is not just key to a tastier brew, in my estimation, but it's also a part of brewing coffee in a realistic way in this day and age.

As I say this, I'm aware that a preference for uniformity in grinding is perhaps a more modern viewpoint, and that my taste for variety might be surprising. However, I think it is valuable to consider what aspects of coffee we found desirable in the past, and to balance them with what these new concepts in grinding have to offer; ideally, this will help us find the best flavor experience for the people for whom we make coffee. Even before we were being ultra precise, excellent coffee experiences were created, so perhaps there is a bigger story to be told beyond the approach of making all grinds the exact same size.

That said, I don't mean to say that a level of uniformity is a *bad* thing. I simply believe that **if we reduce coffee grind particles to a completely uniform size, we also risk reducing the coffee-drinking ritual to a one-dimensional flavor experience.**

What's perhaps most exciting about the tests in this section—and the findings they produced—is that they highlight how much power we have to alter the flavor of our brew by changing our grind profile. In other words, by modulating which particle sizes, and in what quantities, are delivered to the cup, we can largely determine the flavor experience we want to deliver.

And in this way, we're able to cater to whatever preference we—and our customers—may have. If we seek highly identifiable flavors, we can choose a more uniform grind; if we favor complexity and balance, a more varied grind profile will be our call.

Putting this information into action

As my coffee career has progressed, I feel like it has been enriched by an increased understanding of how grind size profile impacts the end cup. Now, when I encounter a new grinder, I'm eager to discover its grind size breakdown, and using the methods we've discussed in this section, I'm able to play around with different combinations of grind size profiles to yield various results in the cup.

I will note that the data I've provided in the tests in this section may not directly apply to the tests you'll conduct on your own—your grind settings and results will differ from mine at least a bit. But what I do think you can gain from my data is seeing a general pattern of how a particular model of grinder behaves. For example, most EK43 grinders likely have a large peak of a single grind size and significantly less of others. If you do an internet search of "coffee grind size graph," you may be able to find this research for your specific grinder model—if it happens to be different from the models I've detailed here.

To put the information we have explored about grinding into practice, you really should have a way to separate grind sizes on your own. You can get something as simple as the Kruve sifter, or as robust as a Ro-Tap sieve shaker (which is not a cheap option). Separating and weighing grind sizes will give you an idea of what you are working with, and will ultimately give you a better understanding of the capabilities and limitations of the grinder(s) you have available.

I hope that experimenting with grind size profiles sends you on a fun sensory experience that deepens your knowledge of coffee grinding!

COMMON FIXES TO GRINDER-CREATED ISSUES

As a barista, it's likely that you don't have direct control over what grinder you use in the cafe, and often must make do with what is on hand. If you find yourself in this situation—and aren't having much success getting your grinder to respond to your needs—I would recommend altering the other brewing factors that are much more in your control, such as water temperature, the brew device and filter, and the brewing variables we'll tackle in Fundamental 4.

On that note, here are a couple of thoughts on how to adjust your brew setup to respond to common issues caused by your grinder:

If your coffee is under-extracted (sour, weak) with a fast transition to over-extracted (bitter, intense) at a finer grind, you should lower your temperature and/or change your brewing device or filter. That sweet spot in the middle is very narrow, but these measures should help you find it. By lowering the temperature, you will have just a little more flexibility to extract before hitting bitter/dry flavors. And by changing the dripper/filter, you will alter the evenness and flow speed of the extraction to increase the chances of hitting your sweet spot.

If your brew is over-extracted and commonly clogs the filter, you may want to try a different filter or lower your brewing turbulence. A more porous, thinner filter will cut down on clogging and improve the water's ability to flow from the dripper, while a lower brew turbulence will slow down extraction speed to reduce over-extracted flavors. Additionally, over-extraction and clogging are indications that your grinder creates too many fines; if your burrs have not been changed (or simply aligned) in a long time, making one of these fixes could also solve the issue.

BREW FUNDAMENTAL FOUR

VARIABLES

For our fourth and final fundamental, I've chosen to focus on three important variables that substantially impact our brew: how we pour our water, our brew ratio, and our water contact time during brewing. I feel that any one of these topics can be overlooked due to the many moving pieces involved in coffee brewing, but ignoring them could come at the cost of not reaching the full flavor potential of our coffee. Without further ado, let's dig into them.

3 IMPORTANT VARIABLES IMPACTING YOUR BREW

POURING TECHNIQUE

The first—and in my opinion the most overlooked—of these variables is the pouring technique, or the method in which we introduce water to the coffee grinds. In this section, we'll cover how different pouring techniques impact extraction and learn how we can use them to bring out the best in our brew.

Turbulence and agitation

As we approach our pouring technique, we must think about the impact our brewing water has as it contacts the ground coffee mass, and the resulting reaction that causes. This can be defined as "kinetic energy," or the energy associated with motion, and it refers to everything from how quickly your stream of water circles around the slurry to the effect of any stirring implement inserted into the brew.

While *thermal* energy is almost always implemented in a brew through hot water, *kinetic* energy can be added to the brewing process in multiple ways and at any given time. The main methods we use to impart kinetic energy are turbulence and agitation. These words are often used interchangeably when talking about brewing, but we'll define them separately, as I view them quite differently. **Turbulence** will refer to the movement of water, while **agitation** will refer to any time you may be manually stirring or adding energy from an external source. We can add a lot or a little kinetic energy to the brew based on how we use turbulence and agitation.

In the brew recipe toward the start of this book, we gave some examples of common pouring methods to introduce this energy into the brewing process. For example, aggressive pouring is a high-turbulence method, where water meets the grinds in a more forceful manner, causing them to mix actively. On the other extreme, an example of a low-turbulence method is slow-flow center pouring, which introduces water more gently to cause less interaction between grinds and water.

While these are just two examples, there are countless variations we can make with our pouring method to affect turbulence. Another important element of our technique is how near or far our kettle is to the slurry when we pour. A shorter pour, with the kettle moving closer to the slurry as the water level lowers in the kettle, will have a gradual lowering of turbulence as the brew continues. Conversely, a higher pour will increase the brew's kinetic energy, though you may lose temperature in the process. (See the sidebar "Accounting for Temperature Loss" on page 76 for more on this topic.)

There are other negatives that can come from longer-distance pours. The further the spout is from the slurry, the more turbulent the water becomes, leading to extra

MORE WATER

- Shallow angle
- Farther from grinds
- Increases kinetic energy
- Temperature loss

LESS WATER

- Steeper angle
- Closer to grinds
- Lower turbulence

incorporation of air into the brew and inconsistent parameters in the extraction. You may notice this when you see splattering of the water hitting the slurry or very large bubbles being formed (note the difference between large bubble formation from splattering versus poorly pre-wet grinds creating excess bubbles during pouring).

Because your pouring approach can have a wide variety of effects on the brew, it's important to control your technique, and to use it thoughtfully to increase or decrease turbulence. With conscious control of your pouring technique, you will be capable of making adjustments to improve upon what you are tasting in the cup.

Testing how turbulence affects extraction

While there are innumerable ways to play with turbulence and agitation, our ultimate goal as baristas is to use these tricks to extract a great-tasting coffee. In theory, a faster pour rate will not only result in more turbulence, but will lead to more water having contact with the grinds, resulting in a faster extraction rate. On the other end of the spectrum, lowering turbulence will slow down extraction speed, resulting in less of an over-extracted flavor. While I find these general pouring theories interesting, I wanted to put them to the test with hands-on experiments to see if the results bore them out.

In these tests in **Figures 15 and 16**, I used three specifically different methods of turbulence and agitation. The "low turbulence" test used simple pre-wetting and a subsequent slow-and-controlled center pour until the desired water weight was achieved. I used enough movement of the stream to ensure full saturation of the grinds, but otherwise kept the turbulence to a minimum. The "average turbulence" test did the same as above, but implemented an aggressive circular pour midway through (with 50g of brew water) to give a stir to the slurry. The "high turbulence" test used fast and aggressive pouring through the full brew, as well as an extra stir with a spoon at the end to ensure maximum extraction.

In the cup, the three samples tasted quite different from one another, and followed the patterns I expected. The low-turbulence brew had a more mild and flat taste in line with under-extraction, the average-turbulence one was sweet and balanced,

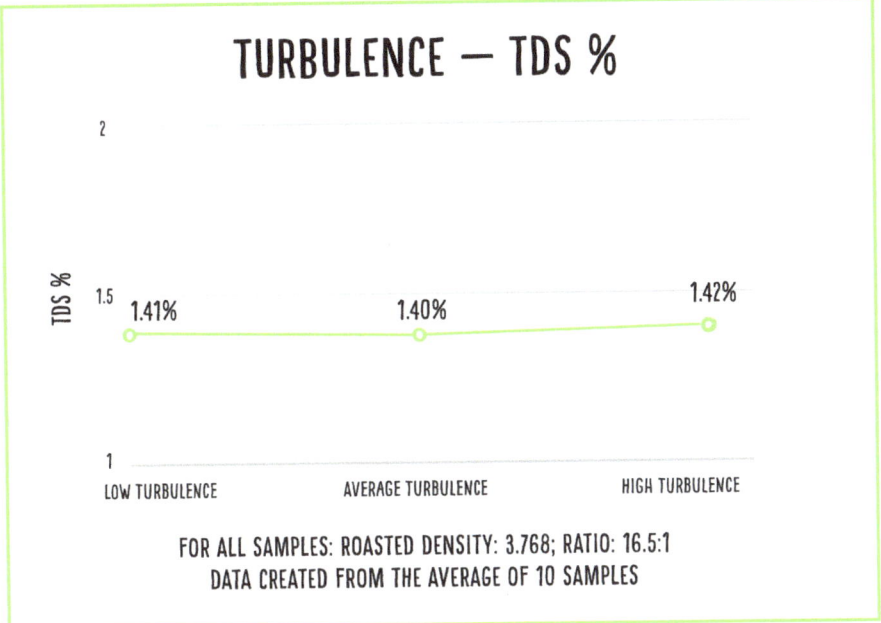

Figure 15

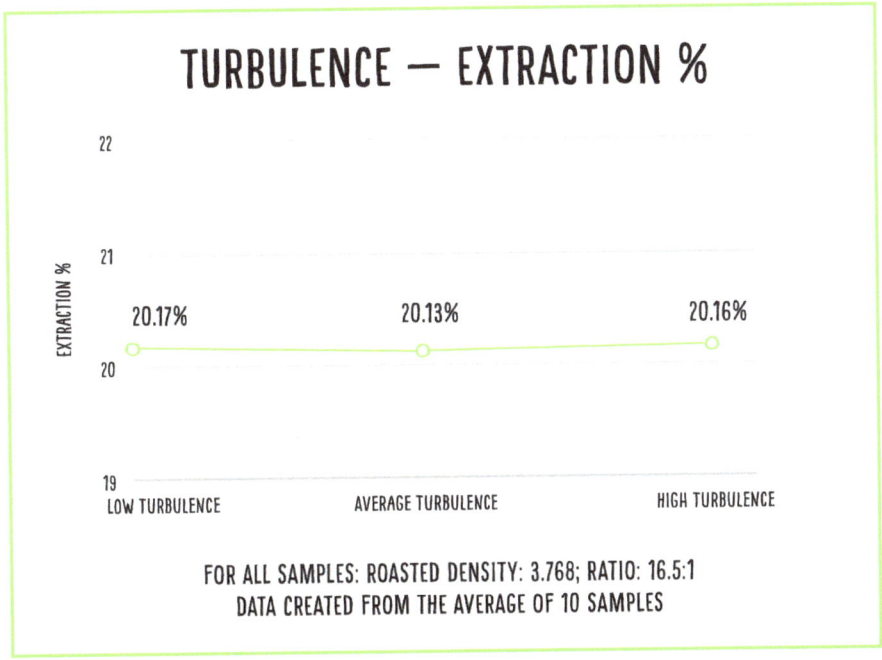

Figure 16

CONTROLLING TURBULENCE BY POURING

High, aggressive turbulence toward the start of the brew, pouring from an increased height.

Lower-turbulence, slow-flow center pouring as the pour progresses.

and the high-turbulence brew had a touch of dryness and bitterness associated with over-extraction. Overall, the brew with average turbulence yielded the best flavor.

However, to my surprise, these brews that tasted so different in the cup showed very little difference in the charts, with quite similar TDS and extraction yield. My best guess as to why this was: Though the kinetic energy caused the brews to extract different ratios of specific components that were noticeable in the coffees' flavor, these elements did not impact the concentration of dissolved solids and the extraction rate.

Pouring technique takeaways

I believe the flavor results from the three turbulence/agitation tests provide us with useful information you can use to determine if you are using too much, too little, or just the right amount of these tactics. The varying flavors show us that you need some turbulence to get the most from coffee, but excessive amounts result in unpleasant, unwanted flavors. I have found the method that has produced the most consistently high-quality results in my brews is high/aggressive turbulence at the beginning of a brew and another moderate amount just before finishing the pour.

To conclude this section, I'd like to add that I find turbulence to be a highly preferable option to agitation. I never recommend stirring a brew manually unless you want to stir the bloom portion to ensure the full wetting of the grinds. Techniques such as picking up the dripper and swirling the liquid at the end, or actively stirring the slurry at various points, seem unnecessary. We can easily get an even extraction of coffee through other means—particularly turbulence—simply by controlling how we pour our water.

BREW RATIO

After pouring technique, I think the next most important variable in making coffee is your brewing ratio. To put it simply, the brew ratio is a measurement of how much water is used per unit of coffee. The most common way we measure this is in gram weight, and to express brew ratio we usually state it in terms of "dry ground coffee dose (g) : hot water poured (g)."

The consensus in the specialty-coffee community appears to be that a brew ratio between 1:15 and 1:18 produces the best outcome. My personal preference for specialty filter brewed coffee is almost always close to 1:16.5, which tends to express a balance between strength and dilution (and is important for articulation of flavor).

It is worth noting that the brew ratio has a direct impact on strength, so a "tighter," or smaller, ratio (as in 15 or fewer grams of water per gram of coffee) will automatically make your brew stronger. I decided to explore this phenomenon further by conducting some brewing ratio experiments in which I kept the dose the same and simply adjusted the brew water amount based on the desired ratio. I based the water temperature on the density measurement from Fundamental 1, and I used the same water pouring technique and other variables as my recipe in the beginning of this book.

You can see the relationship between tighter brew ratios and stronger coffee in **Figure 17**, as the TDS percentage decreased as the ratio went up, which essentially correlates to the amount of dilution gained by the increasing water quantity. This is likely not surprising to you, as it is commonly accepted that a lower ratio equals stronger coffee.

What may be more surprising is the behavior of the extraction yield between these samples (see **Figure 18**). As the ratio went up, we saw an increase in extraction yield up to a certain point (1:16.5 ratio in this case), and a subsequent falling off of extraction yield as the ratio got higher.

This shows that our peak in extraction was not completely connected to brew strength, as both the 1:15 and 1:18 brews had a very similar extraction yield

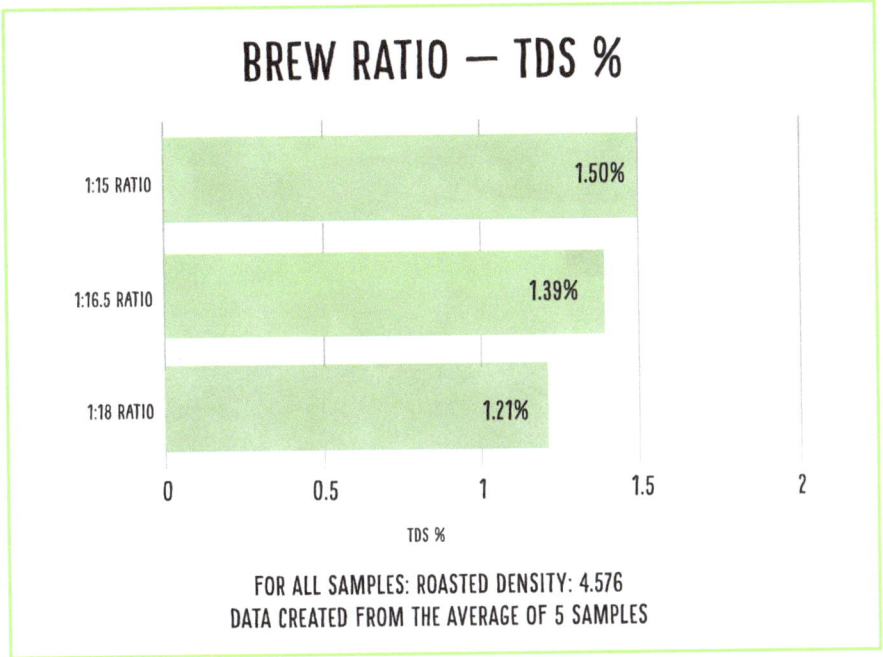

Figure 17

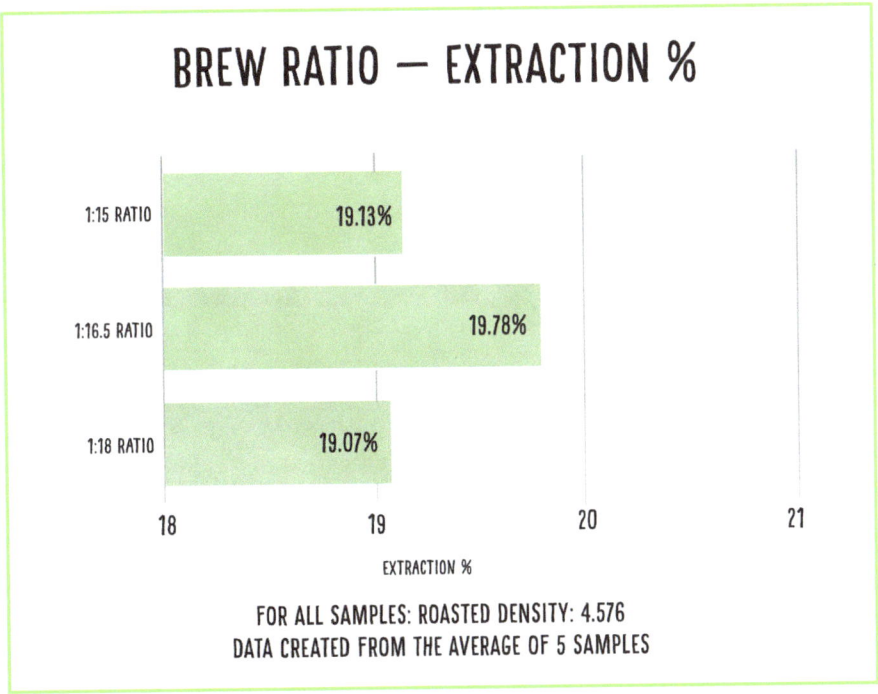

Figure 18

ACCOUNTING FOR TEMPERATURE LOSS

As we covered in Fundamental 1, using the proper water temperature for your brew water is key to properly extracting your coffee. However, it's important to note that the temperature referred to in the density chart in Figure 1 is the water set temperature—the temperature your water should be before dropping to the grinds—and not the temperature of the slurry itself. Unfortunately, our brew water has several opportunities to lose heat between when we start pouring and when we finish brewing.

This heat loss may occur if the water needs to be transferred from one vessel to another before being poured on the grinds, or if the heated water sits for a while before pouring commences. Additionally, the fullness of the kettle will also impact temperature loss. While a fuller kettle will better maintain its thermal integrity and in turn keep the water hotter, it will also lead to the barista pouring the water over the grinds more slowly—and with the spout further from the grinds bed/slurry—to maintain control over the brew process.

This necessity of pouring the water more slowly and farther from the brew provides additional potential for heat loss—in two ways. First, the water must drop further before reaching the grinds, and for every inch (2.5cm) the water must drop, the water loses roughly 1°F in temperature. Second, the thinner the stream of water, the less thermal integrity it will have, meaning it will lose temperature more quickly.

So in order to maintain your water set temperature, you should try to pour with the spout roughly 3 or 4 inches from the slurry surface. This of course is dependent on your kettle not being completely full of water, unless you are using a flow restrictor. I would recommend a kettle roughly two-thirds full, as it provides the thermal stability of increased water and allows for the spout to be closer to the slurry.

percentage, but very different TDS levels. In the 1:15 brew, we simply needed to extract more solubles from the coffee, and in the process add a bit more dilution of water to balance the flavor. The coffee was strong, but not fully extracted, and the resulting brew was sour and quite unpleasant.

The 1:18 brew suffered in a different way, with the full extraction being achieved earlier on in the brew, and a decreased efficiency in extraction as the brew continued. Because I didn't use too high of a temperature and kept the grind the same, the coffee didn't yield its solubles easily enough to continue extracting into the cup. So essentially the brew became more diluted as the extraction continued, and the taste reflected this. It was weak overall, with a very slight grapefruit pith-like bitterness in the finish. The weakness of the brew was further confirmed by it having the lowest TDS reading at 1.21%.

Adjusting brew ratio based on roasting style

Given these results, you may be asking yourself why it might be necessary to change your brew ratio if 1:16.5 worked so well. Once again, the nature of your coffee may be the driving factor here. A change of brewing ratio is most commonly a necessity to accommodate different roast types. Specifically, the extremes in roasting style (both light and dark) tend to fare better with different brewing ratios. Remember that we are already correcting for this variance a bit by changing our brewing temperature via our density chart, but adjusting your ratio is particularly useful when there is no option to adjust the brewing temperature.

Darker roasts are the most versatile in terms of how they may be brewed. At a tighter ratio (say 1:14), the body becomes very heavy and the increased amount of solutes in the cup essentially block the taste receptors, making these brews seem less bitter. Of course, with too dark of a roast, all you will taste is bitterness. On the other side, a "wider," or bigger, ratio (say 1:20) will extract the coffee fully but will add enough dilution that the bitterness in the coffee will become more muted and palatable. This is not so much to say that you should seek out dark roasts for their versatility, but rather that if you find yourself with a coffee that is darker than you prefer, the brew ratio is one easy way to find a more palatable result.

Lighter roasts, on the other hand, are far less versatile. Roasters often give very light roasts to high-grown single-origin coffees, which tend to be very dense beans with high acidity. If you use a tight brew ratio with an already acidic coffee, the result is almost always sour or unpleasant. Rather, I find that a medium brew ratio (1:16.5) will yield a balanced cup from these coffees, given that you have adjusted your brewing temperature appropriately. However, once again if the option to change temperature to the degree needed is unavailable to you, brewing with a wider ratio may be your best solution. In this case (say 1:18), a light, acidic coffee may express itself quite well, as the added dilution spaces out the intensity of flavors and improves the impression of sweetness in the cup.

Outside of the case of roasting, some coffee filters also will see a benefit from a tightened brew ratio. In particular, the Kalita Wave and Chemex filters have tasted

1:15.5 OR 1:16 WORKS WELL WITH KALITA

best to me at ratios of 1:15.5 or 1:16 over the years. I would equate this to the filter tests we did in Figures 7-10 in the Device & Filter section, in which the thicker filters of the Kalita Wave and Chemex resulted in a lower brew yield. By using a tighter ratio when brewing with these thicker filters, we concentrate the brew to help make up for the loss of dissolved solids.

Brew ratio takeaways

In the end, my most common brewing ratio for filter coffee is 1:16.5 for a simple reason: It produces the best results for my palate on a consistent basis. The other variables covered in this book tend to take care of any flavor issues I run into, and adjusting the ratio simply isn't necessary most of the time. So I recommend you start (and stay) at this ratio, and only adjust it if other variables are unchangeable or a new coffee is being finicky.

WATER CONTACT TIME

We started our journey with water, so I think it's only fitting that our last major brewing variable is water contact time, which refers to the amount of time in which the water interacts with the coffee grinds during our brew. This is an important variable that can make or break our cup, so here we will explore how water contact time affects extraction, and how we can establish and adjust it.

Understanding extraction types

Water contact time is counted from the moment that water is poured onto grinds (usually for the bloom), and it concludes when the extraction is considered finished (my recommendation is after all liquid has drawn through the grinds). When it comes to pour-over brewing, we have two separate types of extraction happening: steeping and percolation.

With **steeping**, water permeates the structure of the coffee, reaching cells on the interior of the grind. The coffee's solubles then begin migrating out of the interior and into the liquid solution in which the grinds are steeping (aka the slurry). The more filled with solutes the slurry becomes, the less efficiently additional solubles will extract. Because the liquid is resistant to pulling more from the grinds over time, coffee made with the steeping method is less likely to have an over-extracted flavor. That is not to say that the brew is not strong enough, though—in fact, steeping often leads to coffee liquid that is simply too strong due to the extended water contact time. You just may not hit as high of an extraction yield due to the nature of this action.

STEEPING

In **percolation**, water is constantly being poured onto the slurry and moving through the bed of grinds. As the water washes past the surface of the grinds, it is dissolving and extracting the tiny solubles found in the cells on the exterior of the grind particles (the particles' *exterior* solubles extract in percolation but their *interior* solubles extract through steeping, due to the longer soaking times in the two extraction types). Percolation is a much more efficient extraction method compared to steeping because the water is not becoming oversaturated with solutes before moving toward the decanter or mug beneath it. Fresh water is constantly

PERCOLATION

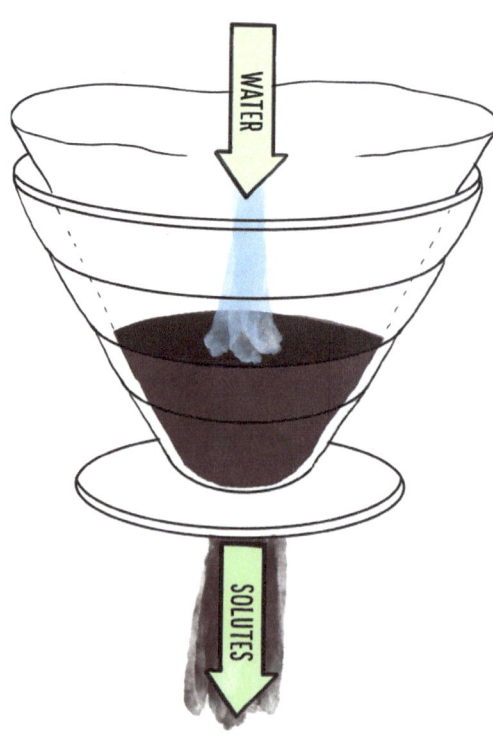

being replenished, continuing the extraction of the grinds without slowing down the rate of extraction. However, this increased rate can lead to over-extracted flavors in the brew more easily than in steeping.

Of course coffee can never be quite as simple as we would like it to be, and while percolation is the primary method of extraction discussed in this book, the truth is that almost all well-made pour-over brews are ultimately a combination of both steeping and percolation. Because we are pouring water into a slurry and the water is in contact for an amount of time before eventually exiting the brew device, the water mixes with the grinds for a short time—steeping them—before filtering through and subsequently exiting the dripper. And as a relevant side note, this is an example of why the aforementioned fine dust is a necessity in brewing to some degree: Fine dust is one of the main elements slowing down how quickly the water flows through the slurry, increasing the water contact time and the opportunity for steeping.

The water-grind relationship

Because you have these multiple interactions happening in a pour-over brew, tracking your brew time is quite important. As the brew time goes up, the water has more time to pull that extra little something undesirable into the brew. We of course also don't want too short of a brew time that causes us to end up with under-extracted coffee, as that is equally as unpleasant.

How long your water contacts your grinds will go hand in hand with the size of those grinds—these two elements are highly interrelated and quite difficult to separate when creating pour-over brews with filter paper. I don't want to over-simplify, but we can reasonably say that the finer the average grind, the less water contact time it should have. Why? Because when there is more surface area for the water to extract from, it will extract faster. Conversely, the coarser your average grind, the more water contact time is needed. Larger particles need more steeping time in order to extract enough solubles (particularly to get enough strength in the brew).

Because the water is constantly moving through the grinds bed in pour-over brewing, it can be difficult to give an obvious correlation between water contact time and grind size in this brewing style. Instead, let's look to French press-style immersion coffee for a clearer example of this relationship, and how changing your water contact time and grind size in concert can affect the brew. The general recommendation for a French press is to use a rather coarse grind and allow the slurry to steep for a long time by coffee brewing standards—typically 4 to 5 minutes. But if you want to try brewing a full-strength immersion brew more quickly, you would likely try grinding that coffee finer to decrease the time needed to saturate and extract the grinds. This should result in a pleasant, tasting, well-extracted brew, though it should be noted that it will be more difficult to separate the grinds from the water with a finer grind.

Water contact time takeaways

So where do you start in establishing the ideal water contact time for your brew? Most specific devices have a recommended brew time range, as well as a general grind suggestion for that device. These recommendations typically come from the manufacturer to produce the best results, taking into account the device shape, filter, and suggested dose amount.

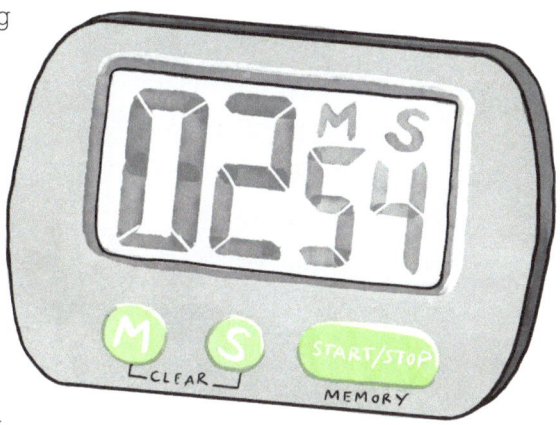

A number of devices and their filters simply do not tend to make great coffee if you deviate from their suggested water contact time, while others are more flexible.

I recommend using that manufacturer's time for the brew device as a starting point, and adjusting from there. In general, I find it best to identify a desired water contact time, and if your coffee isn't extracting the way it should be at this time, you can start looking at changing other variables to improve your brew. Ideally your water contact time will be a steady factor that you can use as an indicator of when it's time to change those other variables.

And when you do change them, keep in mind the aforementioned principle that the finer the grind is for your brew, the shorter your contact time should be to avoid over-extracted flavors. So if your ideal brew time is resulting in over-extracted coffee, you might try grinding the coffee a little coarser for an improved extraction at a similar brew time. Or you might try adjusting another variable like your paper filter—going with a thinner filter should make the liquid flow more quickly and allow less contact time with the grinds, which should improve the flavor.

Brew Fundamental 4: VARIABLES

THE IMPACT OF DOSE SIZE ON THE BREW

While I chose not to include an entire section on how coffee dose weight impacts your brew, I do think this is an important variable to touch on. To explore it further, I conducted tests looking at the effect that two very different doses have on the end product. I took what I had found to be the proper dose to produce a great brew—18g—for one test, and used a much larger dose of 32g for the other. The results were quite surprising, both in flavor and in the data (see **Figures 19 and 20**).

To do these tests, I used the grind setting as described in Fundamental 3, determined the water temperature based on the coffee's density, and used a ceramic V60 with white filters, moderate turbulence, and a 1:16.5 brew ratio. I kept all of those variables the same for the two tests, with the only difference being the different dose amounts, as well as the brew water amount in order to maintain my 1:16.5 ratio. Naturally, the brew took slightly longer to finish (roughly 25 seconds more on average) with the larger dose because there was more water to pour.

Because I had already determined that the 18g dose was a great representation of the coffee, let's focus on the brew made with the 32g dose. It was highly concentrated and too intense in flavor to be considered palatable; all indications were that the brew needed a higher ratio of water to coffee.

Looking at the data, it is clear that the TDS strength and extraction yield increased significantly with the larger dose. This leads me to believe that the ceramic dripper continues its efficiency in extraction as a larger brew continues.

A final note: Because we used more water and coffee with the higher dose, I think the brew would have fared better if we had ground the coffee slightly coarser to speed up the flow of water through the brew, which would in turn have prevented over-extracted flavors.

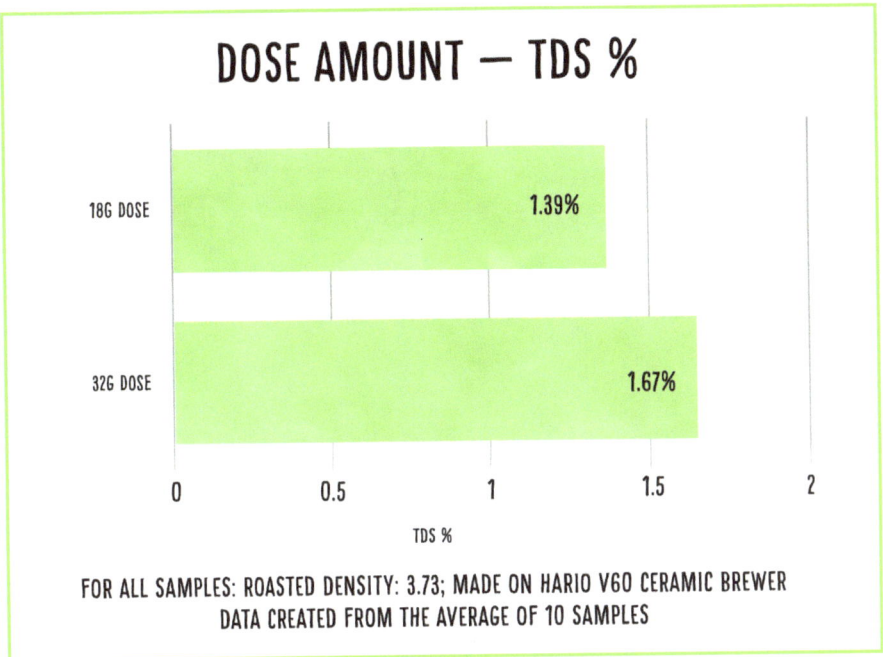

Figure 19

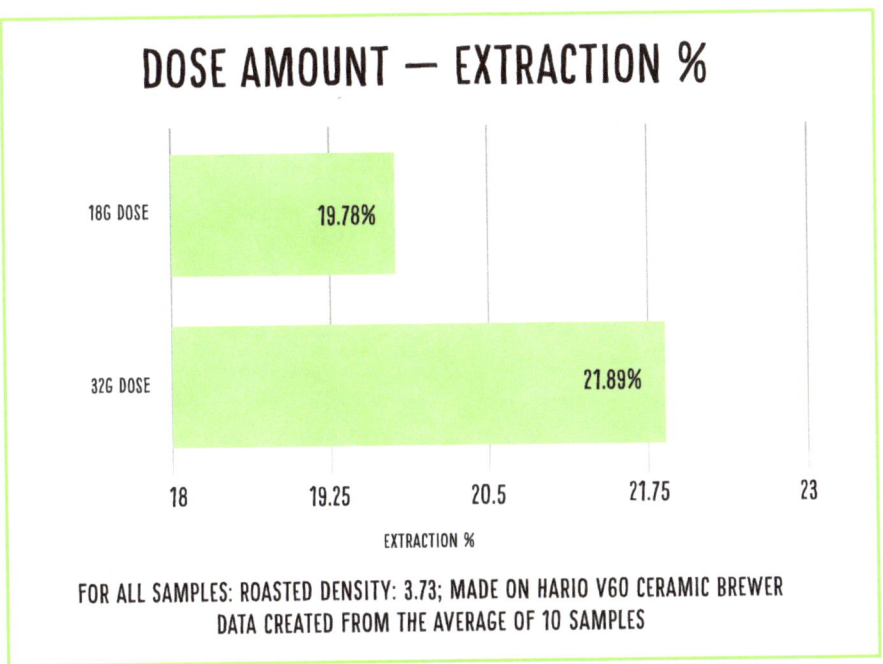

Figure 20

Brew Fundamental 4: VARIABLES

CONCLUSION

HAPPY BREWING

As I think back to that Cafe Show experience I detailed in the preface of this book, despite being out of my element, I was able to use the tools available to me to make great coffee. The roaster's booth was outfitted with a reverse-osmosis system, so the water was an ideal formulation for coffee. If it hadn't been, I had a Third Wave Water packet in my bag as a backup.

I don't generally fly around with a graduated cylinder, so—using an 8-ounce cup and the scale at the booth—I was able to calculate the density of my beans to determine my water temperature, which I set on their variable temperature kettle. They had a Hario V60 and filters, as well as a grinder that cut the coffee to a narrow range of particle sizes to increase complexity in the cup. I used my standard brew ratio and water contact time, and after a few test brews with their coffee, settled on using moderate turbulence to increase extraction.

And I'm happy to report that the coffee turned out great: I made brew after brew resulting in a consistently complex flavor, and the people I met and chatted with really enjoyed it. And also importantly, it reflected well on the roaster who was hosting me at the booth.

It so happened that I only had to make small adjustments from my ideal recipe on that day to deliver great-tasting coffee, but here's the important point, in my view:

I was well-equipped to meet a range of challenges on the brewing front by following the brew recipe—and the principles therein—detailed in this book.

And that is largely what this book is about to me: Putting the power in our hands to make consistently good coffee in a variety of scenarios. Yes, we can make delicious coffee on our home setup with little thought once we dial in a routine. But life happens, and we're not always in the perfect environment—when we're faced with the unpredictable, we have to adjust. And by using the tools laid out in this book, we have the ability to make those adjustments thoughtfully and with purpose. Those tool include not just the brew recipe, but the charts and data sets discussed in this book, which I hope reveal brewing efficiencies and point to methods that yield better results

While the brewing purists in our lives will likely stake claim to a "best" method of making coffee, the truth is that there are countless ways to brew a good cup of coffee. Yes, you may have limitations in some scenarios, but that just gives you license to experiment, and to choose your own adventure in your path to deliciousness—and this book should help you arrive there. Do you have a plastic dripper instead of your usual ceramic dripper today? No problem, just be aware of how that device interacts differently to heat and adjust accordingly. Are you lacking Hario filters for your V60 but have access to some Melitta truncated cones? It may take some filter origami and brewing creativity, but you can still make great coffee. Even if you are in a situation where all of the equipment available is what you like the least, you should be able to apply the principles of this book to make the best brew in your situation. And that is what I want you to have: the ability to make great coffee no matter your obstacles.

Coffee is wondrous in its complexity, but it's also wonderful to know that there isn't just one single way to make it taste delicious. With some creativity and the knowledge to make thoughtful adjustments, we can hit whatever brewing curveball is thrown our way.

GLOSSARY

Agitation. The process of manually manipulating the slurry to saturate coffee grinds during the brew process to increase extraction. This is often done with the use of a spoon or other implement.

Bloom. The degassing process that happens at the start of a pour-over extraction when a small amount of water is poured over dry coffee grinds. A typical bloom formula for filter brewing is 2g water per 1g of dry coffee.

Boulders. Coffee particles that are noticeably larger than other particles during the coffee-grinding process. Boulders are generally defined as being 1,400 microns (μm) or larger in size.

Brew strength. A reference to the concentration of solutes in brewed coffee. Higher brew strength is often a result of smaller brewing ratios and is not directly tied to extraction yield.

Draw-down. The process of the entirety of the brewing water moving through the filter and into the brew chamber.

Extraction yield. The percentage of coffee solubles that are dissolved in brewed coffee. This can be calculated with the formula: (TDS % x brewed coffee weight) / dry coffee dose.

Over-extraction. The result of brew water extracting too many solubles from the coffee grinds, which typically results from the grind being too fine (or the presence of too many fine particles). In the cup, over-extracted coffee is most often recognizable as bitter, dry, or astringent flavors.

Percolation. The action of water moving over coffee grinds, extracting solubles from their surface as the liquid passes through a filter and ultimately exits the brewing device. This is the primary action of pour-over brewing, though elements of steeping also exist in the best pour-over brews.

Refractometer. A scientific tool that can be used to identify extraction amounts and measure the concentration of solutes in brewed coffee. Readings are typically given in the form of a percentage of "total dissolved solids."

Slurry. The mixture of water and coffee grinds in the filter of a device during the brew process.

Solubles. The portion of coffee grinds that are able to dissolve. This refers to compounds that will potentially extract into the coffee solution (but that have not yet been extracted).

Solutes. The portion of coffee grinds that have been dissolved and extracted into the brewed coffee. This refers to compounds that are currently a part of the coffee solution.

Steeping. The action of water and coffee grinds soaking together, allowing the water to permeate the interior cells of the grind, and extracting portions of the solubles into the brew solution. This is the primary action of immersion brewing, though a limited amount of steeping is present in the best pour-over brews.

Total dissolved solids. A catch-all term—commonly abbreviated as TDS—that includes anything dissolved in liquid. TDS is the easiest way to present a snapshot of water chemistry consisting of multiple minerals without getting too in-depth. TDS is also used to convey readings from a refractometer, which is a simple indication of coffee brew strength.

Turbulence. The action of water interacting with the slurry to saturate coffee grinds during the brew process. Intermingling of grinds and water will increase extraction with more energetic action.

Under-extraction. The result of too few solubles being produced from the interaction between water and grinds, and/or when a brew is extracted in an uneven manner. Under-extraction is commonly an indication of the grind being too coarse, or of too few fine particles being present in the brew. A coffee may also be under-extracted if too little water was used, and a highly concentrated brew will result. Under-extraction is most often recognized in the cup as sourness (due to high concentration) or watered-down flavors (due to too few fine particles).

ACKNOWLEDGMENTS

I believe no one rises to a high level without the help and support of others, in specialty coffee or otherwise. So I'd like to take the time to thank a number of coffee friends and family who have helped me grow—and who ultimately led me to being capable of writing this book:

First and foremost, thanks to Masha and Zoey for giving me the time to research and write this book. It has been a long process, and I appreciate your support to get it done. And for helping me take my mind off of writing in between!

To Deb Kaminski and the Pacific Foods team for believing that good people are worthwhile and that helping people is a great cause. And for giving me the chance to write this book in the first place.

To Miguel Meza for being an incredible resource of knowledge in farming, varietals, processing, and roasting. And for taking me on the journey that eventually led to my World Barista Championship win.

To Holly Bastin for convincing me to take a job as a barista in 2003, teaching me fundamentals, coaching me in years of competition, and being supportive over the years and distance. And for just being a great human and friend.

To Taylor Minor and Charles Nick at Third Wave Water for being supportive and working hard to get some lovely magnified photos of filter paper, as well as some grind sieve analysis. And for making brewing water a little less stressful.

To Craig Simon for challenging my point of view as well as adding to my personal coffee knowledge over the years. And for just being able to have a laugh with me.

To Robin Seitz for being a great friend, making me laugh, and sharing "Venti cappuccinos" back in the day. And for making a smoked brisket of legend.

To T. Ben Fischer for being driven by your passions, as well as having a vision of how to bring people together. And for inspiring me when I was feeling old and jaded.

To Tim Wendelboe for inspiring me to pursue greater professionalism and representation of myself. And for that Cuban cigar.

To Heather Perry for showing me that a barista can be more flawless than I ever imagined. And for letting me play *Call of Duty* with Ryan all those nights.

To Maxwell Colonna-Dashwood for pushing the boundaries of what we consider in barista competitions and in coffee professionalism. And for the important input on the water section of this book.

To all of the judges and professionals who judged me or gave me feedback over the years. Without critical feedback, I would never have been able to grow.

To all of the farmers and producers I have met and interacted with over the years. You have inspired me and showed passion and excellence in so many ways. Without your dedication, I would have never had the product to work with that this book is focused on in the first place.

To Cindy Ondrick for bringing her impressive visual flair and stylish illustrations to the book as its designer. And for helping me present my words in an appealing package.

Lastly, to Chris Ryan for editing my words and somehow making me sound much more elegant and refined than I ever feel about myself. And for honest and critical questions that ended up making a far better book than I ever imagined.

There are so many other people who have contributed to my knowledge over the years, and I feel that I learn something from everyone in some way. If you have ever had a discussion with me about coffee or something related to this industry, you have added to who I am. Thank you for being a part of my journey!

ABOUT THE AUTHOR

Pete Licata is the founder of Licata Coffee Consultants and has worked in specialty coffee since 2003. A decorated barista competitor, Pete won two U.S. Barista Championship titles before winning the World Barista Championship in 2013. In his varied coffee career he has worked as a barista, a competition coach (training 2014 World Barista Champion Hidenori Izaki), and in product development, roasting, and coffee quality. A native of the Kansas City, Kan., area, Pete currently lives in Melbourne, Australia, where he works as a research and development consultant for Nomad Coffee Group. For more on Pete, visit **www.licatacoffeeconsultants.com**.

ABOUT PACIFIC FOODS

Pacific Foods is proud to support the production of this book. An active member of the specialty-coffee community, Pacific encourages baristas' professional development and regularly supports events bringing together barista communities nationwide. The company is also the manufacturer of the Barista Series™ line of plant-based beverages designed for professional baristas, and uses the valuable feedback of baristas to perfect its products.

www.ingramcontent.com/pod-product-compliance
Lightning Source LLC
Chambersburg PA
CBHW042051290426
44110CB00001B/21